THOMAS NAST

Political Cartoonist

THOMAS NAST

THOMAS NAST

Political Cartoonist

By

J. CHAL VINSON

UNIVERSITY OF GEORGIA PRESS
ATHENS

To

ALMIRA

CONTENTS

ILLUSTRATIONS

Following the Index

PREFACE

THOMAS NAST, widely acclaimed in his own day and still recognized as one of America's greatest political cartoonists, has been relatively neglected by biographers since 1904 when his personal friend, Albert Bigelow Paine, wrote *Th. Nast: His Period and His Pictures*. This book unfortunately has been out of print for many years. Such an excellent reference service as the Photographs and Prints Division of the Library of Congress has only a dozen or so prints of his cartoons. The main body of his work is in *Harper's Weekly*, but complete runs of those volumes are fairly rare and their unwieldly size makes them difficult to use.

In this book it is my purpose, therefore, to make available to students of American history, politics, journalism, art, and humor in convenient and manageable form a representative selection of Thomas Nast cartoons from the several thousand matchless ones he drew. All contemporary political cartoons, particularly those of Bill Mauldin, Herblock, Oliphant, and "Baldy," interest me. I have been fascinated by Nast ever since I first discovered him while completing a Master of Fine Arts degree under the direction of Lamar Dodd at the University of Georgia. For several years thereafter I collected material to write a biography. It became apparent at length that this would be impossible, for Nast was not a man of letters and no collected correspondence remains. Cyril Nast, his son who was living at the time my research began, confirmed my findings on this matter. I then turned to my present project which has always presented a unique challenge to me personally, both as a trained artist (my present hobby), and as a teacher of history of some years standing.

To recreate for the modern reader Nast's life and the pattern of his artistic development, I have selected and arranged chronologically drawings from each period of his work. I have sought to give enough of the artist's life and the political problems of his time to put the individual drawings into an understandable setting. To a marked degree these drawings are Nast's autobiography. Great effort has been made in the reproduction of the cartoons both as to size and quality to remain true to the original. Some reduction in size has been unavoidable because Nast's favorite format was the oversized single page drawing in *Harper's* which was eleven by fourteen inches in size, and some were double paged—fourteen by twenty-two inches. In any event the drastic and distorting reduction that is necessary in most textbook reproductions has been avoided.

I should like to give special thanks to Cyril Nast for his help in the preparation of this book. The final section on Santa Claus drawings is largely made up of his own favorites from his father's drawings. Included among them is Cyril's portrait (No. 150) as an infant being admired by the good saint.

Especially useful in this work were the biographies of Nast by Paine, already cited, of Oakey Hall by Croswell Bowen, and the Tweed Ring by Alexander Callow. The photographs used for comparison with Nast's portraits were supplied by the Photographs and Prints Division of the Library of Congress. All of the Nast cartoons with the exception of his self-portrait at an easel were taken from the files of *Harper's Weekly*.

I should also like to acknowledge the aid of the late Dr. George H. Boyd, former Dean of the Graduate School at the University of Georgia,

for research time and funds that enabled me to
collect copies of a great number of the cartoons
used in this book. Thanks are also due to Dr.
Joseph H. Parks, head of my department, Dr.
Robert McRorie, Director of Research, and Dean
Gerald Huff of the Graduate School for making
research time available to me for this work. Dr.
John O. Eidson, Dean of the College of Arts and
Sciences, has always encouraged me to continue
my research and writing. Ralph Stephens, Director
of the University of Georgia Press, has been most
kind and helpful in the presentation of all of
my books.

J. Chal Vinson

Department of History
University of Georgia

1

YOUNG THOMAS NAST

THOMAS NAST in the course of his career became far more than a successful political cartoonist— he became a presence, an institution. His public to a degree unequaled by any other graphic artist or any other humorist, with the exception of Will Rogers, waited for his drawings not only for amusement and pleasure but for direction. "Let's wait and see what Tommy Nast says about it," expressed this respect for his insight.

This veneration was won by solid achievement over more than two decades. As a Civil War reporter he was called the North's best recruiting sergeant. As a civic reformer he drove William Marcy Tweed, New York City's most rapacious political Boss, into prison at the point of a pen. As a political commentator he swayed voters in every presidential election from Lincoln's in 1864 through Cleveland's in 1884.

Nast's great achievement was all the more remarkable in that it was unprecedented. No American cartoonist before Nast had sustained an impact on the public over any period of time. Newspapers and periodicals did not carry cartoons as a regular part of their publications. He made political cartooning a respected and powerful journalistic form. It was not coincidental that the "golden age of cartooning" followed Nast, for it was built on his contributions. To a greater degree than any other American caricaturist, Nast broadened the graphic vocabulary of the political cartoonist by popularizing such symbols as Uncle Sam, the Democratic donkey, the Republican elephant and the Tammany tiger. Truly Nast was the father of American political cartooning, for he expanded its scope and established the conventions that brought the art to maturity. As a sort of bonus over and above his influence on public life, he drafted the image of Santa Claus that for more than a century has warmed the heart and continues to excite the anticipation of American children at Christmas.

Thomas Nast was born on September 27, 1840, at the military barracks of Landau, near Alsace, where his father was a trombonist in the Ninth Regiment Bavarian Band. The elder Nast was outspoken in his political views, a dangerous habit in view of the oppressive conservatism of governments in the German states of that time. Tom was only six when the family moved to New York City, where the father joined them when his enlistment expired in 1850. A skilled musician, the senior Nast became a member of the Philharmonic Society and the band at Burton's Theatre.

Tom found New York exciting and pleasant. One of his joys was following the tiger emblazoned truck of the Big Six Volunteer fire company. By coincidence its chief at the time was Big Bill Tweed, later the villain in Nast's greatest drama.

Tom began drawing while a child. From the start his art was a comment on current events. His first exhibited work was a drawing of Louis Kossuth, the celebrated Hungarian revolutionary, who in 1851 received the greatest ovation in New York since Lafayette's triumphal tour of a generation earlier. The picture was praised by Nast's teacher, framed and hung in a place of honor by the principal's desk. This was about the extent of the young German's academic success. Art was his only interest, and even the expedient of changing schools several times did nothing to spur him in his formal studies. "Go finish your picture. You will never learn to read or figure," was his teacher's judgment. The family vainly sought to turn Nast to his father's profession of music or to a trade. Fortunately, however, he clung stubbornly to his drawing and was allowed to study art under Theodore Kaufmann, a German painter of historical scenes, who became his mentor and friend. Then for a time Nast copied such old masters as he could find in the museums of the City and later studied at the Academy of Design.

Though something of an innovator in American art, Nast had a long tradition in caricature to build upon when he began his career with *Leslie's Illustrated Weekly Newspaper* in 1855. Caricature is so ancient an art that it may be traced back to Egyptian papyri carrying lampoons of the high life of the times. It became a part of western culture in fourteenth century Italy in the work of Cristofani Buonamico and quickly spread to France, Germany, and England, reaching maturity in the early nineteenth century. In England it found a particularly hospitable home and became a social and political force in the moral fables of William Hogarth and the political satires of Thomas Rowlandson. The real founder of the still prevailing school of English political caricature was James Gillray, who developed his technique to attack Napoleon between 1803 and 1811. A new dimension was added to the art by John Doyle who eschewed the coarseness and exaggeration of his predecessors and drew faithful likenesses of his subjects. He was the real founder of the "Punch" cartoon developed by his son, Richard Doyle, along with the three Johns—Leech, Gilbert, and Tenniel. A monthly caricature sheet was started in 1830 and with the establishment in 1841 of *Punch*, the weekly illustrated periodical, political caricature was permanently launched in England. Talented craftsmen who now had ready access to a large and enthusiastic public set the style for American caricature and greatly influenced Nast, especially in their use of portraits, animals, and symbols. Typical examples are drawings Nos. 1, 2, 3, 4. Even the use of the word cartoon to describe a humorous drawing was a British invention.

Nast did not owe all of his inspiration to the British. There was, in fact, an American school of cartooning dating back to May 9, 1754, when Benjamin Franklin sought with the first newspaper cartoon—the segmented snake, "Join or Die"—to rouse the colonists to cooperate for defense. In the election of 1800 the Federalist attack on Jefferson included one of the best of the early political cartoons, "Mad Tom in a Rage" (No. 5). Another early work that added a word to the language and helped defeat Governor Elbridge Gerry's bid for re-election in Massachusetts was Elkanah Tisdale's drawing of "The Gerrymander" (No. 6), a fierce-winged, arrow-tongued, sharp-clawed dragon who redivided electoral districts to suit party voting strength. William Charles, a Scot driven from home because of his critical cartoons, admired and copied the work of James Gillray and introduced his techniques into America. Charles made notable use of caricature against the British during the War of 1812. From his first presidential race in 1824 Andrew Jackson inspired many political cartoons. Typical examples are "A Doctor Puzzled" (No. 7) and "Political Quixotism" (No. 8). In the Jackson era, and after, most electioneering cartoons were printed on single sheets (broadsides) and were distributed to voters by eager party workers. The most distinguished work of this type was done by Currier and Ives whose lithographs were issued during each election from 1848 through the Civil War. There was no regular outlet for cartoon publication because only one newspaper, the *United States Telegraph*, carried a series of cartoons and that only for a brief time in 1832.

Though highly original with a very distinct style in its mature period, Nast's work shows at all stages of its development the debt he owed to the English and American pioneers.

In addition to this foundation on which to build Nast had the good fortune to begin his career at the very moment that Frank Leslie, an English engraver on wood, whose real name was Henry Carter, launched under his pen name *Frank Leslie's Illustrated Newspaper*, a sixteen-page weekly selling for ten cents. Here was the market and audience for cartooning that earlier American artists had lacked. Here, too, was an opportunity for a poor boy who wanted a career in art to avoid the grim necessity of starving to death to achieve it. The time was ripe for a master cartoonist to appear, and Nast was well equipped to seize the opportunity. Despite his informal training and his extreme youth, only fifteen, he was able to get work at *Leslie's* for the next three years at a salary beginning at $4 per week and advancing to $7. More valuable than the money, which was paid only occasionally, was the association with Leslie and other competent artists on the staff. Several of these, in particular Sol Eytinge, a capable comic draftsman, encouraged and instructed Nast. During these years he also studied the work of Leech, Gilbert, and Tenniel. Their general style of presentation and use of symbols, such as the British

Lion, the Bengal Tiger, John Bull, and Brother Jonathan (Uncle Sam), were to be evident in Nast's later work. As late as 1869 Nast copied from Tenniel the line drawing technique in which his best cartoons were done.

While learning, Nast was also working. In terms of his later achievement, his most important assignment was a leading role in *Leslie's* attack on the "swill milk" evil. Polluted milk from diseased cows who were milked in filthy stalls was being sold in the city under the protection of corrupt city officials. When Leslie sent Nast and other artists to draw pictures of conditions at the barns, irate dairymen threatened the life of the editor. *Leslie's* persisted in what turned out to be a bitter, fierce, and successful campaign. Nast had his first introduction to corrupt city government and the power of the pencil to combat it.

When *Harper's Weekly* was launched in 1857, Nast determined to join the new sheet. This ambition was not fulfilled until 1862. However, he did publish in *Harper's* a single page of several drawings dealing, prophetically enough, with civic corruption in the form of scandals in the police department. This ended for three years his work with *Harper's* but not his opposition to civic corruption. Encouraged by the success of his police scandal pictures, Nast assailed New York gambling houses in a series for the *Sunday Courier*. Although corruption continued despite these blows, Nast had found his calling.

Soon he was able to get a job with another new paper, the *New York Illustrated News*, at $40 a week, the most he had ever made. Among his important assignments were covering the funeral of abolitionist John Brown and another anti-corruption series exposing the vice and misery of life in the New York tenements.

Evidently his work was well received for his next assignment took him to England to cover a news event so important that it overshadowed the slavery-ridden tension of politics in 1860. This event was the prize fight near London between American champion John Heenan, a blacksmith from Benicia, California, and Thomas Sayers, who as English champion wore a belt said to be worth £100. "Never in the history of nations has there been a sporting event that even approached it in public importance," said one contemporary commentator. Sayer's right hook was admiringly de-

scribed as "the auctioneer" while Americans told in awed tones of how the "Benicia Boy" swung at his blacksmith's forge a 32 pound sledge hammer with one hand. Several efforts were made in England to prevent the fight from being staged. Heenan had to move his training camp three times in eight weeks to avoid arrest, finally setting up at Trent Lock which was located at the juncture of three counties making it simple to escape the jurisdiction of any one sheriff. "Pugilism," American papers explained, "was considered a low and brutal sport by many in England." Even so, the stolid *London Times* unbent long enough to consider in staid editorials the possible outcome of this epoch-making conflict. Charles Dickens was said to have bet on the fight, and William Thackeray later denied reports that he was among the spectators. Prime Minister Lord Palmerston deplored the whole sordid affair, but concluded that if the fight must go on he hoped the English champion would win.

Fight they did, and by the forty-second round Sayers, who weighed 156 pounds to Heenan's 210, needed the protection that Palmerston boasted was every Englishman's right. Police broke up the battle which despite the plight of the British pug, at least as related by American observers, was called a drawn battle. The *New York Illustrated News* devoted an entire issue to the pictorial reports by Nast explaining that pugilism had come to be first in public importance not only in America but also "in the whole civilized world." Unfortunately for Nast the paper was not as generous with his pay as with his pictures. He had gained a measure of fame but was virtually penniless.

Nast had come to the end of one assignment, but another soon presented itself. Early in May, Garibaldi had begun his bid for the liberation of his country with the attack of his famous "Thousand" against the Kingdom of the two Sicilies. The fight for freedom stirred the blood of young Nast who borrowed enough money from prize fighter Heenan to get to Italy in time to join the second expedition, June 9, from Genoa to Sicily. Nast followed the fighting for the next four months, including the campaign for the conquest of Sicily and the capture of Naples. Nast's pen was busy covering every facet of the campaign, and his work appeared both in the *London Illustrated News* and the *New York Illustrated News*.

Most of the next two months Nast spent in travels over Italy including visits to the art galleries and the Coliseum in Rome. Florence, Milan, and Genoa were other stops on his trip through Italy to Switzerland, thence to Germany and his birthplace—the Bavarian town of Landau. More travel took him to art galleries of Germany before he returned to London early in January. There the *London Illustrated News* offered him permanent employ, but the young artist found the weekly pay of $10 unattractive. Then, too, he was anxious to return to America where his bride-to-be awaited. Back in America on February 1, Nast found the *Illustrated News* in such bad financial straits that he could not collect all of his pay; the journal's pride in "our special artist" had advertised his work and built his reputation, however.

The struggle for the Union, which was to become Nast's life-long theme, was his next assignment. On February 19, only a few days after his return to America, he covered Lincoln's reception in New York and followed him to Philadelphia and to Washington for the inauguration. (The great painter Winslow Homer, then an illustrator, reported this event for *Harper's*.) Events moved rapidly. War was declared, and troops were raised. Nast's real career was begun with a picture of the New York Seventh Regiment marching down Broadway on April 19, 1861. A painting the artist made from this drawing hung for many years in the armory of the Seventh Regiment.

The busy artist did not completely devote his time to national events. The day before his twenty-first birthday Nast married Miss Sarah Edwards of New York after two years of courtship. Despite Nast's impetuous outlay—all of $350 for a piano, on credit, as the first piece of furniture—the couple began a long and devoted union. Nast's wife evidently came from a family of culture and learn-ing. In later years she was to inspire much of the literary background for her husband's cartoons, such as scenes from Shakespeare and apt quotations from other writers.

The young man who now sought fame and fortune in New York was short and stocky in build, not unlike the Santa Claus that Nast immortalized in his Christmas drawings. Like St. Nick, Nast usually showed himself as smiling and good humored, a rather disarming pose for a man capable of such tenacious and savage attack upon his artistic victims. In common with Rembrandt, Nast delighted in self portraits and like many another impecunious artist doubtless was his own model when he could afford no other. He is unpretentious in his own cartoons, most frequently appearing as surprised or amused and seldom as shocked or outraged.

Apparently he lived a very quiet life outside of the society that his fame might have gained him. Devoted to his trade, he worked so hard that hand cramps hindered his work in the latter part of his career. Throughout his entire career he was a man of great personal integrity. In an age of scandal, many efforts were made to bribe Nast outright or obligate him by bestowing gifts, but none succeeded. This integrity led him to insist on selecting his own subject and treating it in his own way even when a less severe attitude might have extended his career.

Nast finished the eventful year of 1861 with the *Illustrated News*. Early the next year he accepted a job at $50 a week from his former employer, Frank Leslie. After a short time Leslie, perhaps because of financial stress, cut Nast to $30 a week and let him go a month later.

Experience would do much to perfect his style, but he was equipped already both in temperament and technique to work effectively for a great cause. It did not take long for the man and the hour to meet.

2

CHAMPION OF THE UNION

In April 1861 the fateful shot at Fort Sumter sundered the Union and sentenced the dissident sections to four years of frightful slaughter before "the terrible swift sword" could be sheathed.

Conflict increased the demand for illustrated newspapers and consequently for illustrators. It was not long before Nast was able to get a permanent job with the best known of those papers, *Harper's Weekly*. Thus he began early in 1862 an association which during the next quarter of a century was to carry him and the "Journal of Civilization" to the heights of fame.

Fate had given young Nast an unusual opportunity; with his talent he was to make the most of it. There was promise of things to come in his early work for *Harper's*. Hired as an illustrator, even his literal drawings had emotional impact. They contained an element of comment as well as observation, even though technically crude and quite different from his mature style. Indeed, the success Nast enjoyed was the result of a fortunate meeting of his character and the nation's crisis. The tense, partisan atmosphere of war for Union perfectly suited the young satirist's strong sense of moral conviction and gave full play to the righteous intensity so evident in his best mature work. The artist had no need to worry about his audience; his own feelings were matched by the militant mood of the embattled Union.

A natural soldier whose battle-axe was the pen, he gloried in fierce conflict, for he was "primarily and before all a moralist." Nast's best work was filled with "a flaming sense of righteousness." Delicacy and indirection he never mastered; his avowed purpose at all times was "to hit the enemy between the eyes and knock him down." To be at his best Nast needed a definite and despicable foe to demolish. The Civil War and its aftermath of violence and passion provided both the challenge he was fitted to meet and an enthusiastic audience to cheer his successes.

While largely forgotten now, these early drawings were an important contribution to the Union cause. Just how important it is now difficult to judge. Nast's national fame came to a climax almost a decade after the war. It was easy then for enthusiastic supporters to read his contemporary fame back into the earlier period on the theory that the man who toppled Tweed could have had little trouble with Jefferson Davis. It is true, however, that *Harper's* had the largest circulation of illustrated papers of the time—estimated at over 100,000—and Nast's work was seen by a great number of people. At least one wartime contemporary, Abraham Lincoln, reportedly said, "Thomas Nast has been our best recruiting sergeant. His emblematic cartoons have never failed to arouse enthusiasm and patriotism, and have always seemed to come just when these articles were getting scarce."

Ironically, Nast's job at *Harper's* may have been more the result of expediency than of merit. The war had so increased the public demand for pictures that even Union officers were pressed into service as artists if they had any talent. The journal had to struggle to meet its weekly quota of illustrations. The process of printing was cumbersome and slow. Each drawing, prior to printing, had to be transferred to a block of boxwood for engraving by hand. The engraver cut down all parts of the picture which were to be white leaving the black parts standing to take the ink. So great was the rush in getting pictures ready by deadline that a single drawing would sometimes be divided into as many as four parts so that work could be speeded by having four engravers work on it at the same time. When completed the four blocks would be locked together in a frame for printing. Naturally this urgency did nothing to improve the quality of the art.

Nast had not yet developed his cartoon format and did not use portrait caricature as a standard part of his work until 1867. His stamp is evident, however, in emphasis on the individual and the strong emotional appeal of these drawings. Factual illustration was not an end within itself for him; his drawing, regardless of subject or treatment, tended to be a polemic for the Union.

Nast's first drawing for *Harper's*, beginning twenty-five years of association, was "A Gallant Color-Bearer" (No. 9). Apparently he was well regarded, for this drawing was featured on the cover of the September 20, 1862, issue. It is an excellent example of the way Nast infused his work with feeling, depicting patriotism to the last full measure of devotion and evoking outraged hatred for the murderous enemy. This format of a single picture Nast varied with a combination of several small pictures on a single theme (No. 14). The artist favored multiple pictures to the detriment of his illustration's pictorial quality. Eventually in his best mature work he combined the pleasing artistic quality of a single drawing with the thematic emphasis on the many small works combined in one.

Nast's first half dozen drawings, his entire output for 1862, were sharp indictments of the Confederates—the embodiment of evil in his eyes. Even at the end of the year when he turned to drawings for Christmas, Nast used the sentiment of the season to serve his patriotic purpose. Santa Claus, always dear to Nast's heart and a favorite subject in later Christmas pictures, is shown as a new recruit to the Northern cause dressed out in a suit of stars and stripes (No. 151), distributing presents only to happy Union soldiers. When contrasted with the savagery of his other works, this drafting of Santa Claus seems whimsical. The other drawing, "Christmas Eve 1862" (No. 10), skillfully exploits the emotional appeal in the loneliness and fear of a family separated at Christmas by the war. While it appears somewhat maudlin in its simplicity, it nevertheless caused tears at home and at the front in that less sophisticated day. Nast, however, as the war became more desperate, found little time for sentiment. Except for a soldier shown on furlough in 1864, there were no more Christmas drawings.

The peak of Nast's war output, both in numbers and intensity, came in 1863 when thirty-two drawings, over half his output for the entire war period, reached the public through the pages of *Harper's*. As the year began, the vintage of the grapes of wrath was flowing freely. The blood of heroes shed in lost battles washed away the indifference that had bred a measure of tolerance in the first months of war. It was a time of unlimited violence and Nast, with no effort at objectivity, struck to kill through his medium of pictures. Then, and throughout his career, he saw issues in terms of a moral crusade of absolute right against abject wrong and translated his beliefs into unequivocal graphic statements that seldom failed to stir his viewers.

Nast rode the rising tide of hatred in his continued attacks on Southern atrocities such as "The War in the Border States" (No. 11). Not only did Nast show the grief of a mother and her small children as her husband falls, the victim of a Southern sniper, but also intensified the impact by contrasting these barbarities with a scene showing a kindly Union soldier sharing his meager rations with civilian war victims. He utilized the atrocity theme throughout the war with such telling effect that recruits were won to the Northern cause. His fame spread throughout the South, bringing him a host of threatening letters. One of his friends declared that Nast would have been burned at the stake had he ever fallen into the hands of the Confederates on his trips to the front. While documented instances of Confederates burning anyone at the stake are nonexistent, his campaign was undoubtedly resented by his foes.

In these and in the majority of his drawings of the later war period, the germ of Nast's genius was increasingly evident in the emotional impact of his work. Although many members of *Harper's* staff went to the front to gather material for their sketches, it was the summer of 1863 before Nast abandoned the studio for first-hand observation of the battlefield. Traveling to Fort Moultrie he met General Ben Butler, who later as a politician was the victim of the sharp point of Nast's pen. On subsequent trips to see the troops in action, Nast was invited by General Sheridan to establish headquarters at his camp. Even when at the front, young Nast's descriptive drawings were more notable for feeling than fact. In seeming exceptions, such as "The Result of War—Virginia in 1863" (No. 12), the artist's personal viewpoint is evident. Almost alone among Nast's works it emphasizes landscape devoid of people. This stark picture of destruction seems to go beyond a denunciation of the enemy to condemnation of war itself. So, too, does "The Battle of Fredericksburg" (No. 13) with its close observations of suffering, wounded, and tense emotions of men waiting to go into battle. This chilling commentary on a real as opposed to a glorified battle scene must have cost the Union a few recruits.

Despite these effective drawings in 1863 the artist still frequently followed fashion rather than his own insight in undistinguished sketches of prisoners in camp or armies on the battlefield. Typical of these was the two-page spread "Thanksgiving Day, 1863" (No. 14), offering little either as propaganda or illustration.

While suffering in comparison with Nast's later work, these drawings were well received, bringing him a wide reputation and a number of new opportunities. As the tide of battle turned in late 1863 and early 1864, Nast forgot the war, drew innocuous scenes of such subjects as skaters in Central Park, and devoted much time to illustrating books. As an artist he had succeeded, but as a patriot he had made, it seemed, a small and undistinguished contribution to victory. This, however, was not the case, for his greatest service to the Union cause came in opposing the Copperhead peace movement and reelecting Lincoln in 1864.

Lincoln had been nominated in June without great enthusiasm by a combination of Republicans and War Democrats. The war was savage and slow in mid-1864 and even before the Democratic convention met, a Republican faction began seeking to repudiate Lincoln. Charging that he could not win, they demanded another convention to nominate a new candidate. The breach within the President's party grew worse in July. General William Tecumseh Sherman's drive stalled in front of Atlanta; the Radicals in Congress defied Lincoln's plan for reconstruction. When the Democratic convention met, it adopted the resolution of Ohio Copperhead Clement Vallandigham which called for immediate efforts to end the war and bring the seceding states back into the Union at any price. To many battle-weary Northern voters there was strong logic in this appeal for peace. "Mac Will Win the Union Back" became the slogan of nominee General George McClellan's campaign, even though he repudiated his party's pacifism. The demand for peace brought crisis. Lincoln, it is

now known, wrote August 23: "It seems exceedingly probable that this administration will not be re-elected." One of Lincoln's detractors was District Attorney A. Oakey Hall of New York (later a victim of Nast as Mayor and Tweed Ring member) who accused Lincoln of every "crime in the decalogue."

The magnitude of danger, and possibly enthusiasm over the fall of Atlanta, tore Nast from his book illustrating and back to war with a drawing (September 3 while the Democratic convention was in session) that might properly be called the first cartoon of his mature period. In a drawing as direct and stirring as any he ever made, he ridiculed with savage irony the Copperheads' plea for appeasement—"Compromise with the South—Dedicated to the Chicago Convention" (No. 15).

All that the North had fought for is represented here as defeated—the dead and wounded soldiers of the Union are betrayed. An arrogant Southern soldier, cat-o'-nine-tails in hand and cringing slaves in the background, stands with one foot on a grave. A weeping Columbia bends over the headstone which bears the inscription, "In memory of Our Union-Heroes who fell in a Useless War." The drawing was a sensational success; an increased edition of *Harper's* was necessary to meet the demand. It was reported that during the campaign a million copies were printed as hand bills and distributed. Many other artists dealt with the idea that the Chicago Platform meant surrender to the South. As Allan Nevins has observed, "None of these attacks on appeasement and defeatism had the touch of genius shown in Nast's powerful conception."

Later Nast contributed "The Chicago Platform," which was also widely circulated. It was good propaganda but poor art, for its eighteen separate pictures, each with a long caption, made it more of a written than pictorial document. The artist also stirred the Union Party with a drawing, "Election-Day" (No. 16), November 8, showing soldiers fighting and citizens voting under the caption, "No compromise, Down with Slavery, Down with the Rebels." A final election cartoon, pictorially as telling as "Compromise with the South," although not as widely known, was entitled "How the Copperheads Obtain Their Votes" (No. 17). Over the ghostly protest of a dead Union soldier two Copperheads working by lamplight copy his name on a Democratic ballot from his tombstone. In sharpness of ridicule and utter condemnation of a foe, this picture is as powerful as Nast's later works, for, despite crude technique, his message was clear.

Nast helped win the election for Lincoln. But it was soldiers, not journalists, who pushed Lincoln to victory. The pages of *Harper's* indicated how military events overshadowed politics and political cartooning in the news that reached the public. Less than a dozen cartoons dealt with the presidential race while literally hundreds of pictures of battles and portraits of military leaders were presented. Lincoln's campaign picked up when Jefferson Davis rejected compromise late in August and Sherman captured Atlanta on September 1. Even the most dissident Republicans began to drop their anti-Lincoln conspiracy and abandoned it after Sheridan on October 19 defeated Jubal Early at Cedar Creek. The election of Lincoln, so doubtful in August, was conceded on every side in late October. Even so, his winning margin was a narrow one with a popular majority of only 400,000 out of 4 million votes.

Although people and politicans, both in 1864 and later, thought Nast's contribution to victory was great, he drew only five cartoons for the campaign. Lincoln did not appear in any of these drawings, and Nast did not memorialize the victory with a drawing. Curiously enough only one drawing in *Harper's* recognized Lincoln's election —an elongated Lincoln captioned "Long Abe a little longer."

By New Year's Day, 1865, with Lincoln's re-election and the continued military successes of Sherman and Grant, the crisis of the Union was past. Nast celebrated the coming of victory in a double page drawing contrasting the happy North with the desolate South. With this drawing his war work was complete except for a few uninspired and quite orthodox illustrations celebrating victory and mourning the death of Lincoln. They were artistically undistinguished.

In all, Nast drew about sixty pictures for *Har-*

per's Weekly during the four war years. His work, while professional, was immature and uneven in quality; Nast was not yet a craftsman. Missing was the incisive line and the realistic portrait-caricatures of statesmen and rogues of the time, for the cartoon form and the arresting symbols belonged to the future. Later he abandoned the technique and design of his wartime drawings, and his master works have almost nothing in common with those frequently overcrowded compositions with their undistinguished rendering.

It was 1868 after Nast's cartoons had helped win him the Presidency that General Grant wrote that Nast had done as "much as any one man to preserve the Union and bring the war to an end." Yet, there is ample evidence that Nast's war effort was commended at the time; his reputation as a savior of the Union was not merely the result of the fame he later won. *Harper's* recognized his growing fame by raising his salary. He was able to move to a fashionable residential section and gained such tangible honor as a directorship in a bank. Both his wealth and his ability were recognized in 1869, still well before his greatest days, when the exclusive Union League Club, which had earlier made him a member, presented him a silver vase inscribed to a man of genius in appreciation of "his ardent devotion of that Genius to the Preservation of his Country from the schemes of Rebellion." Perhaps more notable for size than design, it bore a figure of "loyal Art" thrusting a spear into an open-mouthed dragon of secession. This award, of course, may have been more in recognition of his support for Grant in 1868 than in 1865.

He had some impact on the war, and it certainly had a great impact on him. He remained for all of his career an ardent champion of Grant and the Union cause. Throughout the nation bitterness lingered for years providing Nast with a never failing theme of loyalty versus rebellion on which to mount his devastating attacks. It was, indeed, more than a coincidence that the cooling of this war-nurtured hatred and the decline of Nast's career came at the same time.

3

THE END OF APPRENTICESHIP

At the war's end Nast, still only twenty-five, had a national reputation and a secure place on the most important weekly journal of his time. Yet he had scarcely begun to perfect the skill and technique that gave distinction and force to his greatest pictures. In the five years following the war he continued to spend much time on painting and book illustration. This experience was reflected in rapidly improving cartoon technique. Probably the natural emphasis in illustrations on a single idea influenced him to rely in his press drawings on a single picture rather than a collection of several small drawings crowded on a page as he so frequently did in his early work. More important was his adoption of the portrait-caricature in 1865 which soon became the hallmark of all his political cartoons. Finally he turned to line drawing in which he developed a bold and incisive touch perfectly suited to the hand engraving on wood blocks then used. Righteous zeal and instinct for keeping in step with the public mind had always been his. The melding of all these talents brought Nast by 1870 to the full measure of his powers.

Already in 1865 *Harper's* was praising his work and predicting greater success. The editor proudly wrote: "Mr. Nast is already known to our readers. With such eyes and hands it will be a sly, interesting incident or cunning, famous face which escapes proper treatment in the *Weekly*." Two years later the journal again congratulated itself on the skill of its foremost cartoonist, calling him a man of "large artistic instinct" who was pre-eminent in his field, producing drawings which were at once a "poem and a speech." This article was accompanied by a full page portrait of Nast engraved from a Mathew Brady photograph.

The promise of these early years was soon to be fulfilled, for national politics brought him a surfeit of opportunities to exercise his skill in critical comment. The post-war years, the age of hate, brought little surcease from the hostility that

had burned so hotly during the battle. The fight had moved from the field to the forum. As a loyal Union man and Republican, Nast had mourned in symbolic cartoons the death of Lincoln. The assassinated President had not been the subject of any of the artist's wartime drawings, and now that he was gone Nast showed no inclination to follow the fallen leader's ideal of "charity for all and malice toward none." In such drawings as "Which is the More Illegal" (No. 18) and "Slavery is Dead (?)" (No. 19), Nast supported the position of congressional Radicals, led by Thaddeus Stevens and Charles Sumner, that the Negro must be enfranchised in the Southern states and the crime of rebellion punished. This political position Nast held throughout most of his career. Artistically these drawings are also important for they are in contrast to the form he would soon evolve. They reflect his persistent tendency to crowd too many pictures onto one page while relying on long written captions, rather than on the drawings themselves, to express his point.

His artistic maturity began with his drawings of President Andrew Johnson. Politically these are infused with the enthusiasm for the Union, but more important is the first use by Nast of portrait-caricature. Just when and why he turned to this form of art is not clear. The use of recognizable likenesses was, of course, a standard feature of British and American cartooning by Nast's time, but he had used it infrequently. Apparently he had devoted a great deal of time to the study of drawing and portraiture. His ability to draw a "speaking likeness" was remarkable, and it is strange that he did not develop this side of his genius in formal painting at a period when portraits were in great vogue. Among his works for *Harper's* a front page portrait of Grant on July 25, 1863, was his first use of this type of drawing. Two of the drawings for the 1864 election used portraiture. In "Compromise with the South" (No.

9

15), the figure representing the CSA is clearly Jefferson Davis. A later drawing, "The Chicago Platform," featured a portrait of McClellan in the center, and in its many small drawings Lincoln, Davis, Sheridan, Grant, Butler, and other figures are recognizable. A Christmas drawing in 1864 featured a portrait of Lincoln bidding the Southern states to take their places at the National dinner table.

Nast's skill in achieving likenesses was demonstrated in 1865 in a drawing that won a $100 first prize in a competition to illustrate the first front cover of *Mrs. Grundy's Magazine*. Mrs. Grundy was shown on a stage addressing an audience in which about 100 persons, including Nast, may be recognized. The artist must have used a magnifying glass because the drawing is less than six by eight inches with the individual heads scarcely one eighth of an inch in size. When it is considered that the drawings had to be cut into a wood block for printing, Nast's command of his medium is evident.

His steady use of portraiture as a part of what were his first true political cartoons began in November, 1865, with a drawing of Andrew Johnson. Nast's skill in portraiture was sharpened by his work in book illustration to which he devoted much of his time between 1865 and 1868. Portraits were necessary, for example, in his illustrations for the satirical essays on Andrew Johnson's administration, *The Struggles, Social, Financial, and Political of Petroleum B. Nasby* by R. D. Locke. He scored a great public success with sixty life-sized caricatures commissioned as decorations for an elaborate "Opera Ball" given in 1866 at the New York Academy of Music. Eighteen of the drawings were featured later in a double page in *Harper's Weekly* entitled "Grand Masquerade Ball . . ." (No. 20). Among the persons shown are Nast, Horace Greeley, General Grant, Andrew Johnson, and Secretary of War Stanton. These drawings were an immediate success, for portraiture combining utility and decoration had always been the most popular American art form. Recognizable drawings of public figures had an especial appeal in an age when photographs were still scarce. As Nast combined character and personalization with direct presentation of political issues of national concern, the popular response was overwhelming. The demand for his drawings became so great that he gradually abandoned book illustration and de-

voted himself to cartooning. This craft was finding increasing popularity. The *New York Evening Telegram* in 1867 became the first daily newspaper to include cartoons as a regular feature.

Nast's success at this point set the course of his future work. Portraiture made emphasis on personality essential. In all of his best work individuals — Johnson, Tweed, Greeley and many others—were attacked for their personal failings and the issues they represented. Ideas that could not be represented by a particular person were given symbolic forms that tended to become stylized. Best known among Nast's symbols were the tiger representing Tammany Hall (No. 52), the donkey representing the Democratic party (No. 21) and the elephant representing the Republican party (No. 22). (In this cartoon the Democratic party is shown as a fox.) Probably he originated the animal symbols for the political parties, and certainly he made them a part of American lore. In this he followed his English masters who had already developed a rich diversity of symbols, especially the use of animals as representatives of various ideas. Nast, more than any other cartoonist, made Uncle Sam, earlier used by many British and American cartoonists, the now familiar fellow in the striped pants and tall hat (No. 23).

Once Nast developed his portrait technique, he changed and improved it very little in his subsequent work. He usually copied from a photograph as can be easily seen in cartoons Nos. 24, 26, 29, 32, 66, 67, 86, 100, 118. Apparently he did not rely on drawings from life, although he was personally acquainted with many of his subjects. If he made serious portrait studies for pleasure or publication, they have not survived. The slavish use of the photograph, probably dictated by the pressure of deadlines and the emphasis on an unmistakable likeness, is evident in the unvarying position of the head in many drawings of the same subject as may be noted in the series on Tweed and Hall, Greeley, and Blaine. The cartoon of Samuel J. Tilden (No. 25) shows the same head position as does the very different pose in Nos. 25A, 25B.

The literal approach, evident in the first drawing of Johnson, was usually employed by Nast, but the crudity and stiffness of technique also evident in that drawing were eliminated with time. Only occasionally, however, did he force caricature to the point of taking some liberties with the exact features, as he did in the drawing of Ben Butler (No. 26). A more typical caricature was to combine the subject's features with a symbol: for example, the fish body for the face of Hamilton Fish who was secretary of state under Grant (No. 27), the jackdaw drawing of the arrogant Roscoe Conkling (No. 28), the rhinoceros with Blaine's face (No. 138), or Grant as a lion (No. 94). One of the most marked examples of this method is evident in cartoon No. 114, in which the face of Senator Mathews forms a trap. Since it was basic to Nast's technique that his characters be easily recognized, he did not use caricature in the sense of a bold and imaginative exaggeration of an outstanding feature. Nast's caricature was more subtle, with almost imperceptible changes that left the likeness unimpaired, although the expression was wholly changed. A fine example of the artist's methods is the cartoon of Boss Tweed (No. 29). While the face, as the photograph shows, is faithfully copied, the eyes have been made smaller and more prominent, giving an expression of avarice to Tweed's face. His naturally fat figure is greatly exaggerated to carry out the caption's allusion to the giant thief.

Nast brought an illustrator's skill to his task and set a high standard of technical excellence in his best work. The drawings themselves could carry the major story line, but Nast, in common with most American cartoonists, always used captions and frequently over-used them. Typically his whole drawing was littered with comments attached to some plausible prop such as a newspaper in the pocket or a poster on a wall. It really seemed that Americans still did not "trust" pictures by themselves and felt at home with them only when introduced by the more familiar art form of the written word.

With these technical developments Nast was launched irrevocably on his career of satirical cartooning. The portrait made his work highly personal and his approach, in keeping with the craft of satire, was vigorous, independent, fanatical, one-sided, unrelenting, petty, and, not infrequently, in bad taste. These were not faults but virtues, for as Professor Gilbert Highet of Columbia University has aptly pointed out, "Satire in contrast to charity does not suffer long and is not kind. Above all the satirist is a destructive critic. He is able at all

times to distinguish the right from wrong in society and willing to attack the wrong without reservation." Nast's best drawings were those in which he was against an evident menace to society: rebellion, graft, or Democratic presidents. At the zenith of his career Nast's zeal did not repel because he was able to "tell the truth laughing." His pictorial sermons were nearly always entertaining and lively in their unsparing use of ridicule, scorn, mockery, and wit. It was a very difficult and unstable art that Nast mastered for a time. For all of its violence, satire is a delicate art. If it is not done skillfully, it becomes merely absurd.

Nast, while willing to stand alone, had that intangible but indispensable ability, so marked in all successful molders of public opinion, to sense intuitively the public mood. More important, his convictions during his great days coincided with the public's. This area of common agreement is particularly important to a satirist—a critic profoundly angered by the society in which he lives— when working as a newspaper cartoonist. Although his harsh abrasive art is disguised with wit, mass appeal is achieved only when there is complete agreement between satirist and audience as to fair targets for destruction.

Present day comedians, for example, complain that they have few such targets left because their audiences include so many aggressive and organized groups determined to defend themselves from any taint of ridicule. Even forty years ago, humorist Franklin P. Adams remarked that the man-eating shark was the only safe subject for satire, provided the comic was ready to give up swimming. The occupational hazard of the satirist is that he may lose rapport with his public and continue to rage when the mass of men are content to rest. This was to happen to Nast when a public that demanded satire gave way to one that desired nothing more than amusement.

But that day was far off. In 1866 Nast with all the necessary talents for satiric cartooning was presented with the one indispensable condition the satirist can not supply for himself—a fit subject for his wrath. When President Andrew Johnson astounded the Radical Republican wing of Congress by aggressively promoting his own relatively mild program of reconstruction, which did not include Negro suffrage, he was denounced as a traitor and tyrant by his erstwhile political friends.

Nast agreed with this interpretation and found that the readers of *Harper's* accepted it as well. One of the first of these drawings, "Andrew Johnson's Reconstruction" (No. 30), shows Johnson in a Shakespearean setting—a device Nast used much in later years—as Iago posing as the colored man's friend. One of his first political cartoons, it shows a blending of his old and new techniques. The central picture of Johnson and the small pictures below it are cartoons within themselves. The pictures above the center figure and the drawings on either side of it are illustrations in the tradition of his Civil War pictures and not cartoons at all. Then, too, the attempt to crowd seven separate pictures together is a carry-over from the artist's early work.

"King Andy" (No. 31), while ornately detailed, finally brings a single theme, Johnson the tyrant, into focus in one picture. The many figures in the background moving toward the chopping block for execution at the King's command include Senate Radical leader Charles Sumner, abolitionist Wendell Phillips, and at the end of the line, Nast himself. Most elaborate of the Johnson cartoons is "Amphitheatrum Johnsonianum" (No. 32). In this cartoon there are fourteen caricatures in the foreground, and even in the distant crowd the faces of Hoffman, Greeley, Logan, and others are recognizable. Here again Nast uses only one picture. The Emperor Johnson is watching the massacre of New Orleans, a bloody riot of July, 1866, which was interpreted by the Radicals as proof the South was not ready for independent government. Back of Johnson and with head turned from the slaughter is Secretary of War Edward M. Stanton, a Radical sympathizer. At Johnson's shoulder is Secretary of State William H. Seward (note the photographs), and leaning over the front rail is Secretary of the Navy Gideon Welles, both Johnson supporters. In the lower left hand corner Grant restrains the sword arm of a restless Sheridan.

Almost immediately Nast's new, direct, personal assault provoked controversy. George William Curtis, who began a brilliant thirty-year career as editor of *Harper's* in 1866, favored subtle attack by indirect means, a literary technique unsuited to Nast's talent and temperament. His career probably was saved and his unique contribution to cartooning encouraged by Fletcher Harper, one of the owners, who established the firm rule that

there was room on the journal staff for men of differing ideas and methods. Thereafter, Nast could always look to Fletcher Harper for the strong support that a man of outspoken views needed. When Fletcher died in the late 1870's, Nast's troubles mounted and his career began to wane.

Unfortunately, Nast left neither a written commentary on his philosophy of art nor even a body of personal letters reflecting his opinions. Yet his pictures demonstrate his agreement with an articulate modern cartoonist, Bill Mauldin, who believes: "A cartoonist can't really be 'for' somebody." He must find something and "hit" it; an effective editorial drawing must be a slap in the face, not a polite entreaty for attention. Forcing his message on the observer, the cartoonist causes him to remember and eventually to act. In the faith that when public attention is focused on a problem the majority will come up with the right answer most of the time, the cartoonist justifies his exaggerated, personal attacks. In Nast's day, newspaper cartooning was new; it did not become a regular feature in most papers until 1896. The harsh necessities of the craft were not understood by many persons. Nevertheless, Nast, following his instinct, insisted on his independence and gave no ground to importunities by his superiors. Such rugged independence brought a lifelong struggle and, in the end, probably shortened his career.

During the 1860's and 1870's Nast had no problem in finding topics. His power to sway political opinion, suggested by his five cartoons supporting Lincoln in 1864, was confirmed by his series of Andrew Johnson cartoons. These naturally led him into a partisan stand in the 1868 election. As a loyal Union man who knew and admired Grant both as a person and a national hero, Nast shared the feelings of a public that solemnly accepted the slogan "To doubt Grant was as bad as to doubt Christ." Nast looked forward eagerly to the presidential election of 1868. It appeared almost certain that his hero would get the Republican nomination. So great was Grant's personal popularity that grateful citizens had raised enough money to present him with houses in Washington, Philadelphia, and his home town of Galena, Illinois. Not to be outdone, the people of New York gave Grant a check of $105,000. These gratuities he accepted without question as no more than the due of one who "from the hand of adverse fate snatched the white flower of victory."

Anticipating Grant's election by the Republican convention, Nast prepared as a backdrop for the speaker's platform a huge portrait of Grant with the caption, "Match Him." The drawing, concealed until the convention formally nominated Grant, was unveiled to the wild applause of the partisan throng. "The Man Who Saved the Nation" in his letter of acceptance struck a popular if unprophetic note with his admonition: "Let us have peace."

Grant's entry into politics cemented the alliance between Nast and *Harper's*. Book illustrations and drawings for other papers, such as the *Chicago News*, kept his contributions to *Harper's* at a minimum between 1865 and 1868. After Grant's nomination, however, the journal offered Nast a regular fee of $150 per double page cartoon, five times more than his rate in 1862. With the opportunity to help elect Grant and make what was then a fabulous salary, Nast went to work in earnest.

His preparations for his political comments were meticulous. Lacking the benefits of a formal education he sought to make up his deficiencies by hiring college students to read to him at a dollar an hour while he drew. His wife, who also read to him, frequently suggested literary titles for his drawings. One of her first important contributions was the "Match Him" title under the Grant convention portrait. Nast himself read the newspapers carefully, pencil in hand, writing his comments in the margins. Also, because of his prominence in his own field he enjoyed the advantage of meeting most of the important political figures of his time. Yet, he was never a deep student of government—an asset in that he always kept the outlook of his readers.

By important coincidence for Nast's later career, the Democrat's first fully attended national convention since 1860 was held in the summer of 1868 at Tammany Hall's new headquarters in uptown New York. These sumptuous facilities had been built at the suggestion of the Grand Sachem of Tammany, William Marcy Tweed. The somewhat reluctant Democratic candidate Horatio Seymour, six times governor of New York, was sponsored by Tammany's controlling clique. In addition to Tweed it included Peter B. Sweeney

and Richard Connolly. This clique included three-fourths of what was later called the Tweed Ring. The other fourth was the Tammany choice for mayor of New York in 1868, A. Oakley Hall. So loyally was he supported that his landslide went eight percent over the city's actual voting population. These incidents explain why Nast always identified the Democratic party with Tammany and Tweed.

Nast, thinking of Democrats as initiators of rebellion, supported Grant with passionate zeal. Seymour proved to be a particularly apt victim of Nast's rapidly developing skill at caricature. Tufts of hair on either side of Seymour's head became under the cartoonist's pen a pair of horns giving the aspiring Democrat a satanic appearance. When the Democrats accepted the Republican challenge to fight out the campaign on the Reconstruction issue, Seymour's Copperheadism during the war was in marked contrast to Grant's matchless war record. "Vote as you shot" was the irrefutable Republican argument. As was to be his custom in later campaigns, Nast devoted most of his pictures to attacking Seymour and the Democrats, only occasionally stopping long enough to glorify Grant. One of the earliest drawings exhibiting his mature style, the powerful "This is a White Man's Government" (No. 33), depicts Seymour joining hands with the Irish vote and Confederate vote to prevent the Negro from reaching the ballot box. The use of figures to carry the theme with captions minimized and background simplified are typical of his most effective techniques. Incidentally, while championing one minority group, the Negro, Nast made no attempt to conceal the strong anti-Irish bias that remained with him throughout his career. Another campaign drawing showed Grant victorious at Vicksburg in July, 1863, while Seymour, mayor of New York at the time, was condoning anti-draft riots. It was tellingly titled, "Matched." A rumored assassination plot against Grant gave rise to "Wilkes Booth the Second" (No. 34), showing Seymour drawing a sword labeled New York Democrats and, while accompanied by the K.K.K., slipping up on a peaceful Grant.

Despite Grant's overwhelming electoral majority of 214 to 80, the campaign was surprisingly close. California and Indiana came to the General's support by narrow margins. With a popular vote plurality of 300,000, it was estimated that the ballots of 500,000 recently enfranchised ex-slaves swung the election to Grant.

After the campaign, Grant, evidently overlooking these figures, attributed his victory to "the Sword of Sheridan and the Pencil of Thomas Nast." While Nast worked hard for the Republican victory, Grant probably underestimated the significance of the newly adopted Fourteenth Amendment on the election returns from Southern states.

Gradually Nast was acquiring his full powers as a craftsman. Development of technique required time, and although native talent was great, his work load prevented practice on methods alone. Nevertheless, his constant industry and close attention to method improved his style over the years.

The greatest advance in technique came in 1869 with the full realization that line drawing was his real medium. Heretofore, he combined line drawing with shaded backgrounds, producing a diffusion better suited to oil painting than to cartooning. While working on a reply to a cartoon in *Punch* in 1869, however, he became fascinated with the line technique used by English artist John Tenniel and applied it in his own answering cartoon. Occasionally he had employed this technique before in such drawings as "The Tyrannical Military Despotism of our Republic" (No. 35), or "War Calling Napoleon a Friend" (No. 36), but now he discovered in this method full release for his creative powers. From this time on, line drawing, marked by masterful use of cross-hatching and bold strokes, was his form of expression and with it he produced his most famous works. The virility of the drawings now began to reflect in every line the aggressive and unequivocal nature of Nast's convictions.

The long process of preparation was now complete. Equipped both in mind and in method Nast was prepared to meet any challenge. The challenge was not long in coming.

4

TRIUMPH OVER TWEED

IN 1869, the year Nast attained artistic maturity, he began to attack the Tweed Ring with what has been called "the finest and most effective political cartooning ever done in the United States."

The Ring's boss, William Marcy Tweed, was then at the crest of his career. The Boss, a man of "rather commanding presence, who carried almost 300 pounds on a frame just short of six feet," brought to his task a rich background of experience. Among his early jobs were chairmaker, saddler, bookkeeper, fireman, and chief of the Big Six Fire Company. Suave and polite, with abstemious habits, he found his true calling in public service when in 1851 he was elected to the Board of Aldermen of New York City. There was much for an ambitious young man to learn from this group, whose members were called the "forty thieves." Whether or not it was the result of this training, he was elected to Congress in 1853. Retiring from public service for a time Tweed, who was far from being the illiterate oaf he is sometimes pictured, studied law and was admitted in 1860 to the bar. By remitting legal fees on cases for the city government in return for political favors, Tweed gained local political attention and favor of local Democratic leaders in Tammany Hall. They made him Grand Sachem in 1863 and he controlled the organization by 1865. With the help of his Ring, he launched the most avaricious raid on the public treasury in the history of a city not unfamiliar with graft. Completing the Ring were City Chamberlain Peter B. Sweeny, known as "Brains," Comptroller Richard B. "Slippery Dick" Connolly, and Mayor A. Oakey Hall, "O.K." or the "Elegant Oakey" to his friends.

The Ring's major form of graft was the overcharge on construction work. Although for a time the Ring charged a contractor sixty-five percent of his bid for awarding the contract, there was no objection as the overcharge was included in the bid and extorted from the patient people of New York. Best known of the Ring's civic improvements built under this system was the County Court House, estimated to have cost $12,200,000 — reliably appraised afterwards at three million and originally designed to be built for $250,000. Later evidence showed remarkable bills run up on this project including $1,250,000 for plumbing, and $360,747.61 to a carpenter for one month's work.

So smoothly did Tweed manipulate that his take was estimated at $200,000,000 during the next five years. This vast kingdom of graft rested in part on the foundation of all nineteenth century Boss rule — an exchange of jobs and other favors to destitute persons, many of them immigrants, in return for votes. This captive electorate enabled Tweed at the peak of his power to decide the outcome of any city election, which he did whenever it was necessary. He liked to taunt reformers by summing up New York politics in practical terms: "As long as I count the votes, what are you going to do about it?" (No. 37). The city was indeed under the thumb of the Boss (No. 38). Other problems of control could be solved by bribing officials as Nast indicated in his drawing of Tammany's "Brains" (No. 39) and "Gross Irregularity" (No. 40).

The Boss thought of politics as a pragmatic business honored by traditionalists if not sanctioned by idealists. Jobs and favors won more votes than promises and reform programs. Immigrants came in great numbers and landed in New York penniless and jobless. Before they could be useful to Tweed they had to be naturalized so that they could vote. Red cards were distributed at saloons and the bearer was naturalized at a "Tammany" court, sometimes 150 at a time and never with any test. In 1868 alone 41,112 persons were naturalized by Tammany. They thus had confirmed the old world maxim, "It is better to know the judge than to know the law." The Boss looked after them, got their votes, ran the city, and by graft was able to make a public office into a private trust. Corruption was rampant in late nineteenth century America, and Tweed was no more dishonest, only more successful, than bosses in a score of other great American cities. Many sought to match him, but few could equal his record — a million dollars in graft a month for his most lucrative thirty months!

Despite public knowledge of New York City government corruption, when Nast began his attacks in 1869 the Tweed Ring appeared unbreakable. The *Evening Post* and the *Tribune* had attacked it with no success. Tweed was wealthy and few presumed to find fault with a man of wealth in a money-worshiping age. His generous and well advertised donations to all public charities won him the support of the "best" people. The city government's advertising budget was used to muzzle most of the New York press. Eighty-nine papers in and around New York were on this payroll with twenty-seven almost wholly dependent on Tweed for subsistence. Every other avenue of attack was blocked, for elections were controlled while courts and the state legislature were cowed.

Even these apparently all-inclusive security measures did not satisfy Tweed. To make certain that nothing interfered with his bonanza, the Boss, who was a state senator in addition to being president of the New York Board of Aldermen, induced the New York state legislature in 1869 to pass a bill carefully drawn by "Brains" Sweeney and providing New York with a Board of Audit to oversee all city expenditures. Furthermore, the city's four-man Commission of Public Works under the new charter was, by conniving rather than coincidence, Tweed, Connolly, Sweeney, and Hall.

The potential graft that this plan offered was unlimited. In Gotham's garden of corruption where one dollar had grown, it now seemed possible to grow ten. The "honorable" members of the legislature were neither blind to Tweed's purpose nor critical of his ethics; they were eager to share the spoils.

When the charter went before the legislature in September, 1869, Nast's first Tweed cartoon appeared. It was significant not only because it began the cartoonist's most famous series of drawings, but also because its subject matter, the Boss's unsuccessful effort to gain control of the National Democratic organization, identified Tweed in Nast's mind as a national rather than a local political figure. It also identified the Democratic party with the corruption of Tammany Hall. Several more Tweed cartoons appeared before the end of the year. Nast began 1870 with a drawing, "Shadows of Forthcoming Events" (No. 41), a double page spread made up of ten small drawings predicting a dire future for the Ring-ruled city. At the bottom of the page in the center is one of the first drawings of the Ring showing Tweed, Connolly, Sweeney, and Hall as statues on Tammany Circle in Central Park. It dealt with too many diverse topics for it to be composed as a work of art. Nast evidently realized that his subjects had to be selected and shaped to the demands of pictorial presentation. In his continuing campaign he concentrated on the Tweed Ring alone as the symbol of all corruption in New York. Even here, he directed much of his attack on graft against individuals—chiefly Tweed and Hall (Nos. 37, 39, 41, 42, 44, 45, 46).

Tweed, as Boss and nominal holder of forty city jobs, was an obvious target, but Hall was the most important city official in the Ring. The new city charter vested the Mayor with responsibility for all appointments and required him to sign all vouchers for city expenditures. In the event of Mayor Hall's death, all his authority would pass to Comptroller Connolly and thus remain within the Ring. Aside from these duties the Mayor was important because of an unwritten agreement in New York politics. This agreement provided that the office of Mayor be held by one of the "respectabilities" who was on "The List," the social register of the time. Other offices and the graft that might go with them were left to the socially unacceptable. Hall was admirably suited for the respectable role. A graduate of New York University, he studied law at Harvard for a term and passed the bar examination while reading law in John Slidell's office in New Orleans. His wife, being on "The List," was quite aware of her social position. She did not invite Tweed or any of his associates to attend any social affairs that she gave. Hall and Tweed never appeared to be close personal friends. Hall apparently did not contribute to the treasure trove Tweed's daughter received when she married. Later in public testimony Tweed declared that Hall got the smallest cut of the Ring's take. By New York tradition, graft was expected of a Tweed, a Connolly, or a Sweeney, but the Mayor had to appear to be above such chicanery. For this reason Nast often drew Hall with a broom (No. 40), for as a gentleman it was his duty to keep things clean for Tweed. Consequently, evidence that Tweed was stealing was not news, but to implicate Hall would arouse the rich, the wise, the able, and the articulate to do something about reforming city politics. This Nast never failed to do. In nearly every drawing Hall, easily recognized by his glasses, is shown as a part of the Ring. In a number of drawings (Nos. 51 and 59 for example) Tweed and Hall are shown without the other ringmen. In the end it was the people that normally would have supported Hall who overthrew the Ring. All strategic elements aside, Nast found Hall an irresistible mark for a lampooning pen. Highly eccentric and given to extravagant dress in a day that did not insist on uniformity, the Mayor would have been an easy mark even without his beard, long wavy hair, and droopy pince-nez glasses that Nast made famous (No. 56). Even the Mayor's love for puns worked against him. Nast usually spelled Hall as Haul and often drew the Mare (Mayor) as a sick horse (Nos. 46, 56, 60).

There is no doubt of the effectiveness of Nast's attack on Hall. There is some question of its propriety. In the newspapers of that day a man was presumed to be guilty until proven innocent, in reverse of the judicial process. Hall's biographer, Croswell Bowen, believes that it is impossible to get closer to the truth of Hall's role in the Ring than to say that he was "compliant, and had become muddled." He was a man of unique talents and varied interests who was editor of the *New York World* and a very successful lawyer in London after his days with Tweed. Hall insisted on his own innocence and even wrote and acted in "The Crucible," a play about a man unjustly accused of crime. When Lord Bryce published the first edition of his classic, *The American Commonwealth*, Hall sued for libel because of a description of his role in the Tweed Ring. The suit was not brought to trial, but Bryce spent a great deal on legal fees and eventually revised the chapter containing the reference to Hall. Nast was unmoved by any of these events and during the proceedings over the libel suit wrote a letter to the *New York World* condemning Hall. Hall answered Nast personally,

and the cartoonist sent both letters to Bryce as an exhibit in his defense.

Hall who was devoted to oratory, writing, and press interviews gave Nast additional material for cartoons. One example was the Mayor's typical attempt to laugh off charges against him with the remark, "It will all blow over." Nast made this a caption of several effective cartoons.

Nast centered most of the rest of his attack on Boss Tweed who because of his weight in person and politics was well known to New Yorkers. He is shown in cartoon No. 42 with his new City charter. The rumors of City Hall graft and corruption under this charter grew more frequent in the fall of 1870, and Nast stirred the public with some of his best drawings. When the Ring's books were declared "correct and faithful" and free of any malfeasance, Nast drew three leading members of the committee as "Three Blind Mice" (No. 43). It was rumored that a threat to increase assessments on committee members' real estate had made it difficult for them to find flaws in Connolly's bookkeeping.

Tammany swept the 1870 election despite Nast's continued cartoon protest. As yet his drawings had not changed things, but they had not gone unnoticed. Tweed, unaccustomed to opposition, was irritated. When Nast caricatured him in January, 1871, with his hand in the public treasury and his huge $15,500 diamond stickpin, exaggerated until it was as big as Tweed's head, protruding from its place on his ample stomach (No. 44), the Boss' patience was exhausted. "I'll show them damned publishers a new trick!" he said. The trick was to reject all Harper Brother's bids for schoolbooks and destroy $50,000 worth of Harper's books already on hand. New books were then purchased from the New York Printing Company, a corporation belonging to the Tweed Ring.

This was a heavy blow, and the directors of *Harper's* almost collapsed under it. A policy meeting was called and a long debate ensued. Just when it appeared Tweed would win, flagging determination was strengthened and the tide was turned by Fletcher Harper. Disgusted with his colleagues, he got up to leave saying as he went, "Gentlemen, you know where I live. When you are ready to continue the fight against these scoundrels, send for me. Meantime, I shall find a way to continue it alone." Fletcher was called back and finally carried his point—the crusade continued. Nast on May 13, replied to Tweed's book order with cartoon No. 45, showing the Boss knocking a Harper textbook from a child's school desk and cuffing the child. On the blackboard of the classroom was written:

HOFFMAN WILL BE OUR NEXT PRESI-
    DENT
SWEED IS AN HONEST MAN
TWEENY IS AN ANGEL
HALL IS THE FRIEND OF THE POOR

The new textbooks supplied by the Ring's company were entitled *Honest Government* by "Sweed," and *Arithmetic* by Connolly.

Having failed to silence his critic by economic pressure, Tweed sought to restrain Nast by law. As a part of a school-tax levy, mention was made of "an artist encouraged to send forth in a paper that calls itself a 'Journal of Civilization' pictures vulgar and blasphemous, for the purpose of arousing the prejudices of the community against a wrong which exists only in their imaginations." Mayor Hall, in his paper *The Leader*, called Nast the "Nast-y artist of Harper's Hell Weekly—a Journal of Devilization."

Nast's campaign was helped in May, 1871, when Tweed could not resist making a boorish display of his wealth in celebrating his oldest daughter's marriage. The fabulous gifts Mary Amelia Tweed received were catalogued in the public press with such emphasis on cost that a London editor asked whether all the gifts had arrived at the bride's home with the price tags intact. Even if this had not been the case, a general estimate of value could be made. Sweeny gave the bride a reported $40,000 worth of jewelry, and other friends were generous enough to bring the total to $700,000 and bear comparison with the crown jewels of England. With a $10,000 a year limit on city salaries it was obvious that Tweed and his friends must have been supplementing their incomes from some source.

Exact evidence as to the source of all this wealth was soon provided as the result of a series of accidents. The County Auditor was killed in a sleighing accident in March, 1871, and a bookkeeper named William Copeland was employed. As he later testified in court, he found that some ledgers were kept from him and out of curiosity

contrived to see them covertly. They held, he found to his amazement, the records of the Ring's gross graft in construction work. He turned them over to his friend, Sheriff James O'Brien, who immediately realized their value. O'Brien, who at the moment was dissatisfied with his share of the Ring's loot and $12,000 in debt to the Boss, sought to clear himself on both scores by using the information to shake down Tweed. The Boss would not do business and neither would the newspapers. After some weeks O'Brien went to Louis John Jennings, editor of the *New York Times*. The Sheriff remarked that Jennings and Nast had had a hard fight against Tweed. The editor, somewhat discouraged at the moment, replied that it still was a hard fight. To which O'Brien answered, "I said you *have had* it," as he put the transcriptions from Connolly's books on the editor's desk.

Jennings found the material so fascinating that he stayed up the rest of the night reading it. Six days later on July 8 the *Times* began its exposure of the Ring's frauds by asserting that the evidence was too overwhelming to be denied even by the eighteen daily and weekly New York papers gagged by Ring patronage. Nevertheless, New York's most prominent editors were not convinced. William Cullen Bryant of the *Post* disparaged the *Times* and *Harper's* crusade, and James Gordon Bennett's *Herald* called them "Humbug Reformers." Greeley of the *Tribune* aroused Nast's special ire by his adamant refusal to see fraud in the Ring, especially in Mayor Hall. In one of the first of what became his most savage series when Greeley ran for President the next year, Nast drew Greeley standing in tears over a sick horse whose face is Mayor Hall's (No. 46). In Greeley's pocket can be seen a copy of the *Tribune* with the headline: "You lie. Everybody lies except H. G."

Three days after the *Times* launched its exposé the Ring suffered another blow. A bloody riot broke out between the majority of New York Irish who were Catholic and the Ulster County immigrants who were Protestant when the latter attempted to hold a parade celebrating the Battle of the Boyne with their traditional Orange Day ceremonies. The Irish Catholics, Tammany men all, threatened violence if the parade went on as scheduled. Mayor Hall or the Ring bowed to this pressure, declined to offer protection, and ordered the Ulstermen not to march. Intervention by the

Governor reversed this decision, and the march began under heavy military guard. Violence broke out. One policeman and one soldier were killed along with thirty-one citizens who had been watching the parade. This carnage brought great public indignation against the pro-Irish city government. It was suggested that a memorial be built to these casualties and engraved with the words: "Murdered by the Criminal management of Mayor A. Oakey Hall."

Nast, who had served in one of the military regiments called out for the parade, struck at Hall and the Ring with a cartoon on the riot called "Something That Will Not Blow Over." It was filled with savage, fighting Irishmen with grinning baboon faces. Nast was uniformly anti-Irish, but on this occasion he must have felt amply justified. After the riot he turned more to his attack against Hall. In this he was joined by the *Times* with such vigor that Hall sued the newspaper on August 21 for libel. However, he made no move against Nast.

Tweed became so alarmed by these developments that he sent Connolly to *Times* publisher George Jones with an offer of $5,000,000 to quash the story. Jones remarked that not even the Devil would pay that much for him, but he refused the offer.

It was evident gross thievery had taken place, but who was responsible? Nast mocked Ring members' wounded innocence when charged with theft in one of his best cartoons of the series. "Who Stole the People's Money?" (No. 47) depicts the members of the Ring and other city officials standing in a circle and each answers the question by pointing to the man nearest him.

New Yorkers by this time were irked enough to seek a more definitive answer. A group of leading citizens organized on September 4, 1871, a Committee of Seventy headed by Joseph H. Choate, Charles O'Connor, and Samuel J. Tilden, who was a member of Tammany Hall. Tilden's role in this reform movement helped him win election as governor of New York and Democratic nomination for President. Hall bravely averred in the face of this new development, "It will all blow over. The gusts of reform are wind and clatter. Next year we shall be in Washington." Nevertheless, Ring members sought to place all responsibility for graft on Comptroller Connolly whose books had led to their troubles. This demonstration

of the honor that exists among thieves angered Connolly so much that in a desperate effort to save himself he went to Tilden and the Committee of Seventy with additional evidence against his former henchmen. As the legendary New York Irishman was wont to remark, "It is everyone for theirselves." Nast's attack became even more vehement as the case against Tweed took documented form. Diligently he worked to make the public aware of the enormity of the crime and arouse it to action. His work was masterful in stirring the emotions of citizens who had their heads filled with facts by the *Times*. Tweed grew to fear Nast's cartoons. "Let's stop them damn pictures," he shouted after seeing "Who Stole the People's Money?" "I don't care so much what the papers say about me—my constituents can't read; but damn it, they can see pictures!" The pictures in *Harper's* reached 160,000 subscribers and the actual readership was probably several times that number. Its illustrated format gave it appeal to many persons who never looked at the other papers.

From this platform, armed with satire and ridicule, Nast zealously worked to raise the spectre of doubt in the hearts of Tweed's strongest supporters. In August, 1871, even before the drawings had unseated Tweed, *Harper's*, in a feature article, proudly described Nast as "the most cordially hated man in New York at the present day—hated by men whose friendship would have been dishonor." The editor added along with a full page engraving of Nast that he was the foremost caricaturist of the day: "Every stroke of his pencil cuts like a scimitar."

When these drawings began to stir public response, Tweed gave a more exact estimate of Nast's work. Threats of violence were made; Nast was told that continuing the fight against Tweed would cost him his career and possibly his life. These threats failed to intimidate him and the Boss turned to his most trusted weapon—bribery. A lawyer friend of Nast mentioned that a group of wealthy business men wanted to send him to Europe for art study. The artist immediately divined the true nature of this offer and calmly played a waiting game. Pretending interest he drove the price from $100,000 to $200,000, and finally up to $500,000 before refusing to drop his campaign against the Ring with the statement, "I made up my mind not long ago to put them behind bars and I am going to put them there." His friend left with a warning to be careful that the Ring did not get him first. Nast did move his residence out of the city to protect his family but made no other concession. The bribe offered Nast was one hundred times the salary of $5,000 *Harper's* paid him in 1871.

Nast continued in the fall of 1871 his remorseless series of assaults against the Ring. After the Orange Day riots he attacked the Catholic tie of Irish Democratic members of Tammany as in cartoon No. 48 where he raised the issue of public versus private schools. The political threat of the Catholic church was not an infrequent theme in all of his work. *Harper's* felt called upon to explain that Nast was not anti-church, having been raised a Catholic, and opposed the church only when it ignored the proper separation of church and state and dabbled in politics. Irish, Catholic, and Democrat were evils individually and collectively in Nast's eyes. Since Democrats courted votes by failing to enforce restrictions on saloons, the cartoonist often showed rum along with romanism and rebellion as Democratic traits long before the Reverend Samuel Burchard coined that phrase in 1884.

Tweed was Nast's symbol of corruption. He transformed the respectable and dignified Sachem of Tammany, the great and generous man of wealth whose gifts were lavished on charity, into a fat, pompous, vulgar, and grasping thief who was at once ridiculous but menacing. One of his best efforts is "A Group of Vultures Waiting for the Storm to Blow Over" (No. 49). From left to right the Ring's members are Sweeny, Tweed, Connolly, and Hall. With almost diabolical skill Nast took the very marks of respectability and success that Tweed cherished, such as his huge and expensive stickpin, and made them the symbols of greed and crudity. Under these hammer blows the dignity of office and the protection of pretension were lampooned into liabilities. Nast made it possible and then popular to laugh at the Boss; laughter drove out fear, and the public saw the unmasked Tweed as a scoundrel not as a hero. Indignation mounted. The Ring was in peril.

Panic mounted within the ranks of the Ring. The Grand Jury October 19, 1871, began hearing charges against Mayor O. K. Hall. Six days later the charges of personal graft were dismissed al-

though he was found to have been careless and negligent in not examining the 39,257 purchase warrants that passed over his desk in two and a half years. Nast greeted this news with a drawing of Hall's face superimposed on a very sick horse. The caption read: "Our Mare still Lives" (No. 56). (New York was then suffering from a terrible plague on horses.) Tweed ignored the public outcry against him and refused to withdraw from the race for state senator. It began to appear that Hall's prediction might be right—it would "all blow over."

The Ring was indeed far from finished. Nast at this critical moment just before the November elections redoubled his efforts. In "Next" (No. 50) he depicts John H. Keysers, a poor but honest plumber, returning $650,000 in graft to the city while Tweed shows his own pockets are empty, and Hall thoughtfully reaches into his pocket to see if there is anything there. The liberty of counting anyone Tweed chooses in the voting list is the point in No. 51. The climax of Nast's campaign and probably his most famous drawing was "The Tammany Tiger Loose—what are you going to do about it?" (No. 52).

The election of November, 1871, cost Tammany its majority in both Houses of the State Legislature. The only successful Tammany candidate was Senator Tweed. Nast found some small solace in pointing out that the Boss' majority was only one-third of what he had expected (No. 53). Ignoring this exception, Nast produced one of his best cartoons, "Something that Did Blow Over— November 7, 1871" (No. 54). The reference here, of course, was to Hall's haughty prediction of a few weeks earlier, "It will all blow over." The Ring members are shown reeling in the ruins of Tammany Hall. To the far left is Connolly pinned to earth by an empty safe; Hall is at the top of the picture clinging to the shattered remains of a wall; Tweed is in the center where efforts are being made to revive him, while Sweeney is fleeing the scene with a bag marked brains.

Repeated use of simple, ear-catching captions, such as this one, gave Nast's cartoons continuity and produced a devastating cumulative impact. It was a major reason for his eventual success in ridiculing Tweed as a public figure and destroying him as a person.

At this point the Ring began to break. "Brains" Sweeney suddenly decided to satisfy a longtime wish to travel in Canada. "Slippery Dick" Connolly, already the victim of his own cronies, was forced to resign under threats against his life by unpaid city workers and left in some haste to see the sights of Paris. When Hall was replaced by A. H. Green, Nast showed Hall ill in bed protesting that he did not want to be cured by taking a dose of that horrid "Green Stuff."

A few days later "Senator" Tweed was arrested. But as Nast recorded in "The Arrest of 'Boss' Tweed—Another Good Joke" (No. 55), the law still seemed weak. This same idea was carried out in "Can the Law Reach Him?—The Dwarf and the Giant Thief" (No. 29). Nast predicted, with great accuracy as it turned out, that a jail could not hold Tweed (No. 57). However, Mayor Hall was indicted a second time, and the reform Committee of Seventy drafted what it hoped would be a corruption-proof charter. Another heavy blow at the Ring was Governor Hoffman's 1872 decision to attribute all corruption in New York City to Tweed. Nast mocked this falling out of old friends with a parody on the assassination of Julius Caesar (No. 58).

The Ring ceased to be a political factor in 1872. Despite Hall's efforts he lost office, resulting in the seating of a new mayor and board of aldermen. Nast celebrated by showing the long "sick Mare" being dropped into the river as a dead horse (No. 60). Hall's second trial ended in a mistrial and a third hearing in 1873 brought acquittal. "The Finger of Scorn" (No. 59) represented Nast's effort to make the best of this decision. Never again did Hall hold public office, although he protested his innocence until his dying day.

On other fronts little progress was made. Nast in "Justice Blind" (No. 61) returned to his satiric best in protesting the continued failure to punish Tweed. The corruption-proof charter devised by the Committee of Seventy was approved by the state legislature, but Governor Hoffman reverted to form and vetoed it. Finally, Tweed was brought to trial and although defended by $460,000 worth of legal talent including Elihu Root, later secretary of war and secretary of state, was sentenced to twelve years in jail. He languished in a finely furnished cell at Sing Sing prison for a time before

abusing his unusual privilege of daily carriage rides about the city by escaping to Cuba and Spain.

Nast was to salvage one triumph from these failures. When the Boss was traced in his flight to Spain, Alva Adee, who was then American minister to Spain, found a Nast cartoon and turned it over to the legal authorities to use in identifying Tweed. Within a short time he was identified and arrested. They thought that Tweed was a kidnapper as the drawing showed him as a giant holding two small policemen in one hand, interpreted by the Spanish to be children. After being returned to the United States, the Boss still did not give up. Although sick and penniless he sought to have the city's $20,000,000 judgment against him dismissed in return for a full confession of the Ring scandals. His written confession was not accepted on this basis, and Tweed stayed in prison until his death in 1878. The confession did fall into the hands of reporters who published it. One interesting revelation was the division of spoils. Contractors kicked back 65 percent of what they were paid. Of this graft Tweed took 25 percent; Connolly got 20 percent; Sweeney, for all his brains, got only 15 percent, and the Oakey Hall 5 percent.

In a sense "it all did blow over." The Ring members other than Tweed were not broken by their righteous opponents and evaded punishment, although the Ring ceased to exact its toll on New York taxpayers. Even this accomplishment had its flaw for one cynic remarked that the most lasting effect of the fall of Tweed was the lesson in caution it taught to later New York politicians and a score of bosses in other American cities. These details escaped the public. To the people Nast was the hero who had destroyed Tweed; virtue had triumphed over vice. Nast had been the first to challenge the Boss, had refused to be turned aside by pressure or presents, and had not stopped until his foe was jailed. More than any other event he covered, Nast's Ring series helped to arouse public opinion. The Ring lived by the sufferance of an apathetic public, and Nast did a great deal to break the apathy.

Tweed was always Nast's symbol of achievement, appearing in 1886 at the very end of the artist's career (No. 146). The Ring, the tiger, and Tammany Hall, scene of the 1868 Democratic national convention, were inseparably linked in the

public mind by Nast's drawings. He lost no opportunity to make political capital out of the
identification. Nast was still busy with Tweed when
in 1872 election campaign got under way. The
cartoonist used the Tammany tiger as a symbol
of the Democratic party, the still dangerous and
rebellious party of defiance, the party of municipal
corruption. This latter characteristic was especially
useful to Republicans in the 1872 election as the
shadow of scandal fell across the honest soldier
in the White House. The donkey became the Democratic party symbol largely through Nast's drawings, but these came in the late 1870's. Earlier he
had used the donkey as a symbol of stupidity applied to many individuals and to the Greenback
political party in particular.

A further link between the Ring's fall and the
1872 election stemmed from Horace Greeley's attitude toward Tweed. The editor of the *Tribune*,
already working for presidential nomination, did
not want to offend Tweed. He angered Nast by
waiting to condemn the Ring until there was little
doubt about its corruption. Nast once sought to
force Greeley, whose opinion carried great weight,
to action by showing him applying whitewash to
Mayor Hall. The cartoonist was harsh in his judgment for Greeley's *Tribune* followed *Harper's* and
the *Times* into the crusade before any other paper.
When Greeley became the Liberal Republican and
Democratic candidate for President against Nast's
hero, Grant, the artist never tired of showing
Greeley and Tweed as confederates (Nos. 46, 62,
63). These cartoons were the first of Nast's most
furious series of presidential campaign caricatures.
He also used Tweed many times in the 1876 campaign (No. 64).

In the opinion of his contemporaries Nast's
series on Tammany and Tweed "constitute a distinct epoch in American political caricature. He
was unlike any caricaturist who had preceded him,
and his successors have not followed his methods.
He gave the satiric art of caricature a power that
it had never before known in this country, and
seldom in any country. . . . Nast stands by himself,
the creator of a school which not only began but
ended with him."

When the newness of political cartooning in
the United States and the youth of Nast, still in his
early thirties, are considered, the triumph was
even more remarkable. Americans loved results;
Nast's work, in the popular mind at least, had the
direct result of breaking up the most corrupt ring
in New York history and ending a most brazen
exploitation of the people's treasury.

The crusader and the craftman met in many of
the drawings of this period. In the Tweed series
his presentation became increasingly clear and
compelling. There remained, nonetheless, marked
unevenness in artistic quality. "Shadows of Forthcoming Events" (41), on the one hand, reverts
to the crowded format of the early works. On the
other hand, the famous "The Tammany Tiger
Loose—'What are you going to do about it?'"
(No. 52) is excellent in every respect. When contrasted to the same setting as used in cartoon No.
32, President Johnson in the Coliseum, the artist's
development toward powerful simplicity becomes
apparent. "Who Stole the People's Money?" (No.
47) is a classic portrayal of "buck passing"—a
condemnation as sharp and yet amusing now as
when Nast created it.

5

PRESIDENT MAKER

NAST cartoons, because of his marked ability at portrait-caricature, were nearly always personal in emphasis. Fortunately for him the presidential elections from 1864 to 1884 centered on personalities rather than on complex issues and thus were tailored to his abilities. When the candidate's personality was well defined, as was true of Greeley or of Blaine, Nast was at his very best. With colorless figures like Garfield and Hancock, he had more difficulty, but partly overcame it by making these candidates the symbols of their party's virtues and vices.

Through 1876 he was especially blessed in the continuance of Civil War fervor—loyalty to the Union and hatred of treason. "Scratch a Rebel and you find a Democrat" was a standard Republican slogan. Robert Ingersoll, the most famous orator of his day, caught the popular mood in the North when the Republican convention of 1876 cheered to the echo his assertion: "Soldiers, every scar you have on your heroic bodies was given you by a Democrat. Every scar, every arm that is missing, every limb that is gone, is a souvenir of a Democrat." Here was the ideal emotional climate for Nast's cartoons, the conviction that the republic was safe only when guided by Republicans. Extreme manifestation of these feelings was evident every four years at election time. After 1876 personalities and issues became increasingly blurred. The Republican party began to fall into factions, finally splitting when liberal Republicans—the mugwumps—refused to back Blaine after the party nominated him in 1884. As the Bloody Shirt faded into the background, politics became less absorbing, for there was no single issue on which public attention might focus. Nast sought unsuccessfully to meet these changes. Apparently he survived breaking with his party in 1884 by making one of his most brilliant series of drawings against Blaine. This triumph was a final flare with Nast rapidly fading out of the public view. He could not make clever comments on everyday manners and morals; oratory rather than small talk was his forte. When the public tired of his martial airs, he was unable to take up chamber music. His art depended on a public incensed over issues; losing that, he fell into comparative obscurity.

Nast was at the zenith of his powers in 1872. His fierce impatience with clearly discernible foes was matched by a direct, uncluttered drawing style of explosive impact. Wholly wrapped up in his work, he turned out drawings at an amazing rate, producing more than 150 for *Harper's* during the year. He was always at his best in times of crises; events of national interest elicited his finest efforts. A number of drawings still dealt with the Tweed Ring, but Nast's major interest in 1872 was Grant's bid for re-election as President. This campaign was Nast's greatest in the role of President-maker.

Grant always remained, in Nast's eyes, the honest soldier—the savior of the Union. In the same large measure that he venerated Grant, Nast wholly despised all of the General's detractors. "As Soon Doubt Christ as to Doubt Grant," seemed to Nast a reasonable slogan. Nevertheless, rumors of corruption in Washington were rapidly being confirmed by fact. Democrats, unhappy over Tweed's identification with their party, demanded that Nast impale Republican malefactors on the same sharp pen that skewered the "Boss." Nast still believed in Grant's absolute honesty and dismissed most charges of corruption as malicious efforts to discredit the President: "Anything to beat Grant."

Also important to Nast's success was the complete harmony of his views with those of *Harper's* editors. They wrote in April, 1871, that abuse of Grant originated with Democrats who "can not forgive his victory over the rebellion." "The greatest of national disasters," the editor asserted, would be "the restoration of the Democratic party to power."

Republican leaders respected the cartoonist's influence. When he visited Washington in the summer of 1872, he received every courtesy at the hands of his hero, General Grant. There were rumors that Nast was paid for promoting the Republican cause so lavish was the entertainment given him. Nast needed no inducement to support Grant.

Another incentive was provided him by the Democrats who, recognizing the veto-getting power of cartoons, imported from England a well known draftsman, Matt Morgan, to match pens with Nast. Morgan went to work for *Leslie's Illustrated Weekly Newspaper*. In a typical drawing, "Grant's Strategy" (No. 65), he shows the General blowing soap bubbles at Greeley. The bubbles are charges that are supposed to knock the editor down, but, of course, burst when they hit him. Another tried to put the onus of Tweed on the Republican party. It showed Grant in the costume of a contemporary ne'er-do-well stage character, noted for fraud and tricks, dancing to Tweed's hand clapping beat. In the background is a stuffed ballot box. The stylistic similarities between Morgan's and Nast's work indicate the strong influence of the early nineteenth century English cartoonists on their successors on both sides of the Atlantic. A lively campaign followed between the two caricaturists.

These challenges incensed Nast and account in part for the vehemence of his campaign work. Then too, Horace Greeley, chosen by the Liberal Republicans and Democrats, a "conclave of cranks," to head their presidential ticket, while highly esteemed for great personal journalism as editor of the *New York Tribune*, was highly eccentric and a perfect mark for any caricaturist. He was the "homespun intellectual who looked as if he had slept in his clothes and prided himself on being a hick farmer in a sophisticated city." His lack of modesty lead one contemporary to call him "a self made man who worships his creator." He was a cartoonist's dream with his moonface fringed with mutton chop whiskers, his small steel-rimmed glasses, tall white hat, flowing white coat, and green umbrella (No. 66). Such a distinct personality almost defied serious presentation in pictures. In addition to these physical peculiarities, Greeley was without doubt very dogmatic, querulous, and erratic in his opinions. He was not, how-

ever, as charged in the heat of the campaign, an atheist, a communist, an idiot, and a free lover. His definite and outspoken positions on controversial issues brought him trouble, for his political judgment was frequently unsound. To rectify such errors he swung not infrequently to the opposite opinion. Consistency was not one of his virtues; it was easy for Nast to refute Greeley's position in 1872 on many issues by quoting editorials from past years. His party's attempt to challenge Republican reconstruction policies so soon after the war was a great handicap to Greeley's campaign, for the bitterness of "the age of hate" still poisoned the national mind. Republicans demanded: "Should the cause won on the battlefield be lost at the polls?" "Grant beat Davis—Greeley bailed him." Compared to Grant, the nation's saviour, Greeley was made to appear no better than a bumbling symbol of treason.

Nast, in this made-to-order situation, faced one problem. Leaders of the Liberal Republican movement included Charles Sumner, Carl Schurz (No. 24), and a number of respectable Union men. Their criticism of Grant Nast interpreted as a part of the politically inspired "anything to beat Grant" campaign. Furthermore, disagreement on foreign policy had made Grant and Sumner bitter personal enemies by this time. Accordingly, Nast attacked Sumner as sharply as he had censured the Senator's erstwhile foe, Andrew Johnson. "The Last Shot of the Honorable Senator from Massachusetts—He Pulled the Long-Bow Once Too Often" (No. 67) depicts Sumner breaking his bow in attempting to launch an arrow of "Malice-Hate" at the White House.

So harsh were the cartoonist's strictures that they alarmed George William Curtis, *Harper's* editor, who had never liked Nast's savage personal attacks and begged the artist to hold his fire. Well aware of Nast's power, Curtis argued that editorials would be forgotten but "a picture is a blow beyond recall." Unrestrained attack was justified against the moral reprobate Tweed, but not when directed at Sumner, an honorable public servant despite his political views. The editor felt Nast should make distinctions and use good humored satire as well as outraged denunciation. Failure to do so would show lamentable lack of "moral perception." Nast would not and probably could not take this advice. Had he developed this light touch he might have had a longer career since there are more opportunities to amuse than to arouse the public. But without being quick to anger Nast would have made little impression on the nation or on his profession. He seems never to have considered changing his style. Although his direct denunciations were to cause him increasing trouble with editors, his real interest seemed to be in finding a forum that would allow him free scope, never in modifying his convictions to fit an accepted pattern.

However much Curtis wished it to be otherwise, American political campaigns have not provided models for polite and gentlemanly conduct. Exaggeration and simplification have always been basic tools for any able campaigner, whether on the stump or in the press. Fletcher Harper, who understood the problem and knew Nast's value to the *Journal,* sided with him. Curtis gave up his attempt to impose his ideals, and the artist again enjoyed full freedom in the choice and presentation of his subjects.

Rather than relenting, the cartoonist returned to his work with a fury that grew more savage as the campaign reached its climax (Nos. 68-73). Opposition papers dubbed *Harper's* the "Journal of Degradation"; Nast himself was the subject of near libelous caricature.

He did all that he could to make Greeley appear ridiculous and to impugn his character as well. The editor remarked that he did not know whether he was running for the Presidency or the penitentiary. An excellent example of Nast's infinitely detailed style is "The New Organ—(we beg the 'Tribune's' pardon)—ization on its 'New Departure'—Anything to get Votes" (No. 74). Whitelaw Reid, a *Tribune* associate and supporter of reform Republicanism, is shown as an organ grinder, playing "The Bonny Blue Flag" and "Erin Go Brach," as his monkey, Horace Greeley, begs for votes in the Democratic headquarters from Tweed, Sweeney, Hall, and Connolly of the Ring shown in the picture just back of the rail. Upstairs in the window is Andrew Johnson standing beside a hooded figure marked KKK. From the monkey's suit pocket sticks a copy of the *Tribune* with the headline: "What I Know About Getting Votes." This last device Nast repeated

in nearly all of the Greeley cartoons. In fact, Greeley was shown adopting all the evil aspects of the Democratic party. In drawing No. 75 he is linked with New York's Irish Catholic Democrats that Nast so abhorred, and also with rebellion in "The Whited Sepulchre" (No. 76). Here Greeley climbs a ladder, held by Sumner and Schurz, in order to cover with his white overcoat the monument of Democratic infamy based on slavery, the Tweed Ring, Tammany Hall, and a long list of war atrocities. The Liberal Republican slogan of peace with the South and the Union, in fact as well as name, Nast lampooned in the cartoon "Let Us Clasp Hands Over The Bloody Chasm" (No. 77). It showed Greeley shaking hands with survivors of the Union soldiers who were victims of the legendary atrocities in Andersonville Prison. These were harsh indictments, but for Nast politics was war— winning was all that mattered.

Gratz Brown, Greeley's running mate, was ridiculed even more unmercifully. Unable to find a photograph of Brown to copy, Nast drew a tag on Greeley's coat and marked it "And Gratz Brown"; his face never got into the campaign. This was such an apt presentation of the inconsequential office of Vice-president and Brown's personal obscurity that it was immediately popular.

Grant won an overwhelming victory, and Nast's contribution to it was universally recognized if not universally acclaimed. Greeley died only a few weeks later, crushed, so his friends said, by the unmerciful ridicule Nast had heaped on him. One of Nast's last campaign drawings gave credence to this slander. In the background was the *Tribune* masthead bearing the words, "The Cheapest Paper in the Union." In the foreground a prostrate Greeley was being carried away on a stretcher. It was called "We are on the Home Stretch" (No. 78). By singular and unfortunate coincidence the day this drawing appeared, October 30, Mrs. Greeley died. Her death, loss of the election, and old age rather than Nast's abuse were the probable causes of Greeley's death. More tangible evidence of his influence on the campaign came from grateful Republicans. The party through Hamilton Fish, Secretary of State, offered Nast a lucrative sinecure as official American Commissioner to the Vienna Exposition. Even though Nast had already planned a trip to Europe, he refused. Another of his Washington friends, N. P. Chipman, started a testimonial fund for Nast of $10,000 to be raised by $100 subscriptions. Hearing of the plan, the artist vetoed it and the program was dropped. Even at the home office his work in the campaign was noticed. His salary had reached the handsome figure of $18,000 for 1872, almost four times the salary of the Congressmen he lampooned in so many of his drawings and only $7,000 short of President Grant's pay. Even at this pay scale *Harper's* feared Nast might draw for other publications and acquired exclusive rights to his talents in 1873 with a retainer of $5,000 a year to be paid whether he made any drawings or not. For each picture he was to get an additional $150 with no limit on the number that he might produce. When those figures are multiplied by four to give them current value, Nast's financial position becomes clear.

Another marked tribute to his national reputation was $10,000 offered from Redpath's Boston Lyceum for a speaking tour. Nast was no public speaker and, in fact, was terrified at the prospect of addressing an audience, although he finally consented to try. So great was the fame of the man who had beaten Tweed and broken Greeley that the lecture tour drew good crowds and was extended several times, finally running for seven months with Nast collecting $40,000.

Still only thirty-three, Nast was a veteran of eighteen years experience and had reached a peak of influence from 1870 to 1873 probably unmatched by any other cartoonist before or since. He was, as *Harper's* proudly said, the "Prince of Caricaturists."

Yet the path from the peak must be downward and there were signs in 1873 that decline was setting in. That year he began to suffer cramps in his right hand, the price of the almost incessant work of the preceding years. In addition his general health was not good, causing him to be away from his drawing board for some months. Even more important a subtle complacency born of success was taking hold of him. Wealth and fame brought distractions that interfered with his work. A trip to Europe and the Redpath lecture tour took much of his time in 1873. The old urgency, economic and idealistic, was lessening; his output of pictures decreased sharply. He was somewhat like

a musician of limited repertoire—after such fabulous success what could he do for an encore?

This became so evident in 1873 that James Gordon Bennett of the *New York Herald* jestingly proposed a subscription fund for the indigent artist who had given up drawing and was seeking to make a living as a minstrel man singing "Shoo, Fly." Nast answered with the small drawing "Shoo, Fly" (No. 80), showing himself batting at the fly, Bennett. Nast also replied to Henry Watterson, famous *Louisville Courier-Journal* editor, who made much of the artist's absence from the press. The elaborate and amusing cartoon, "Meeting of Nast and Watterson in Central Jersey" (No. 79), parodied the then sensational Stanley-Livingstone meeting in darkest Africa. When these cartoons began to appear, even a rival paper, *The New York Daily Graphic*, honored him with a front page cartoon, "Mr. Thomas Nast at Work Again." It was not vanity alone that caused Nast to picture himself in many of his drawings. As these incidents show, he was a national figure whose opinion on the policies of his time carried weight. Frequently he included his picture in drawings (Nos. 81, 82, and 83), for his purely personal reaction to events was in itself news.

Nast dealt lightly with his vacation, but there was much unconscious irony and prophecy in another self portrait of this period entitled "Our Artist's Occupation Gone" (No. 82). It showed him, hands in pockets, with nothing to do as the news of Grant's victory is announced. While he produced much good work in the next decade and remained a power in the nation's politics, it is clear in retrospect that the great occasions best treated by his grand manner were coming less frequently.

Especially troublesome to Nast was the increasing confusion of issues. The way of a reformer who was loyal to Grant was difficult, especially during the second administration. Corruption in Washington had never reached the peak recorded during this "Era of Good Stealing." An honest politician was cynically described as one who, when bribed, would not sell out to a higher bidder. The Credit Mobilier, with the aid of Congressmen bribed with stock that paid up to 80 percent interest a year, fleeced the nation of $20,000,000 while paying its chief operators 348 percent profits.

Even Vice-President Schyler Colfax accepted twenty shares of this stock and some dividends. But this was only one of a number of scandals. Congressmen raised their annual salaries from $5,000 to $7,500 with the increase retroactive for two years, a $5,000 bonus in the celebrated "Back Pay Grab" of 1873. The Secretary of War, William W. Belknap, was indicted for making a $24,000 profit by selling shoddy supplies to the Indians; in the downfall of the Whiskey Ring, Grant's personal secretary, Orville Babcock, escaped only because the General loyally supported him.

Nast denounced these scandals, but the cartoons were neither as specific nor as numerous as those that condemned Tweed. The "Back Pay Grab" was condemned (No. 84). He turned loose his full force in condemnation of Belknap in drawing "It Struck (In Blowing Over)—Picking Even the Poor Soldiers' Bones to Feather Their Nest" (No. 85). Nast, whose father was an army man, always championed the military forces and here attacked Belknap not so much as a thief as an exploiter of the Army. In general, the cartoonist was no more faithful than the President in carrying out his command: "Let no guilty man escape." So myopic was his view of Grant that he showed him as a bulldog guarding the Treasury from Wall Street manipulators in the drawings "Keeping the Money Where It Will Do the Most Good" (No. 86), and "Every Question With an Eye only to the Public Good" (No. 87). In the latter drawing Justice questions the right of "The Saints of the Press," who themselves have not infrequently betrayed the public, to cast the first stone at Congressmen accused of the Credit Mobilier scandal. In this distinguished group of journalists Nast included his old Tweed Ring adversary, Oakey Hall, holding a paper marked "Star Forger." Again in "This Tub Has No Bottom to Stand on" (No. 88) Nast shows Justice lifting the tub of "Public Corruption" and causing its bottom, "Tammany Hall 1872," to drop out along with "Treasury Frauds," "Credit Mobilier Frauds," "Canal Rings," "Whiskey Rings," et. al. Probably his best defense of Grant, and one of his most powerful single drawings, shows the President (No. 89) as a lion being fitted with a scapegoat's head by his enemies. The fox who

is placing the head stands on the Democratic donkey.

The cartoonist devoted much of his time to other issues—an attack on the demon rum in drawing No. 90 or a comment on foreign policy in drawing No. 91—but these themes did not carry the excitement or elicit the popular approval of his war on Rings or on rebels. The Bloody Shirt, while fading, was still an applause inspiring symbol. Nast rang in this well tested theme with such drawings as "Halt," showing Justice with the sword of the Constitution protecting the rights of the Negro in the South (No. 92). Another in this vein showed Southerners on "The New *Alabama*" raising a skull and crossbones flag marked "This is a White Man's Government." It was captioned "Same Old Pirates Afloat Again" (No. 93). Currency inflation was a live issue in the 1870's but had not stirred the fervor it would arouse in the 1896 "Battle of the Standards." "A General Blow Up—Dead Asses Kicking a Live Lion" (No. 94) represented Grant as a hero defending sound money. In a series of involved puns the "Fine-Ass Committee" of Congress surrounds the President, who had defeated a move toward inflation by a veto, shown as a lion standing by a sign marked, "I will fight it out on this line if it takes all summer" —his famous phrase of the 1864 military campaign. Inflation was also the subject in "Holy Murder!!" with Tilden repudiating inflation for the Democratic party platform by strangling the "Ohio Rag Baby" symbol of soft money (No. 95). The Rag Baby symbol was another Nast innovation which became a standard part of all cartoonists' vocabulary. Still another issue was use of tax money to support parochial schools. Nast, who was consistently anti-Catholic, opposed the policy in a drawing showing the "U. S. Bulldog" (U. S. Grant) guarding the public school treasury. His bias was also evident in "A Legitimate Question About Home Rule" (No. 96).

Nast, in his unceasing defense of Grant, vehemently refuted the *New York Herald-Tribune's* charges of Caesarism—a third term for Grant— made early in his second administration: "Our Modern Canute at Long Branch" (No. 97). Again the cartoonist was on shaky ground, for Grant seemed so willing to serve a third term that the House passed, by 233-18, a resolution condemning the third term as a dictatorial practice. Grant did not seek the nomination in 1876 and Nast's loyalty seemed vindicated. However, the Stalwart wing of the Republican party, sought only three years later, to build up a demand for Grant, put his name before the 1880 convention, and came very close to nominating him on the first ballot. Nast, heretofore, had always been outspoken and always on the winning side of clear cut issues. The issues seem clear enough today, but in his loyalty to Grant, Nast refused to see them. In defending Grant, Nast was further handicapped in that his most effective work was always in attack rather than in support of man or policy. He was not objective enough to use caricature for its own sake rather than to promote a cause. Thus he lost a golden opportunity to shame corruptionists in the "Gilded Age." The field open to him was narrowing, but with the coming of the presidential election of 1876, and the Democrats' selection of Samuel J. Tilden of New York as their standard bearer on a reform ticket, Nast was back in business. A vulnerable target for his partisan attacks, Tilden had attracted national fame as one of the destroyers of the Tweed Ring. Nast was not among his admirers. Tilden was a Democrat, and Nast felt he had entered the fight only when it was certain that Tweed would lose. As prosecutor he had failed to convict Hall. The artist capitalized on Tilden's membership in Tammany Hall and the rumors that "Slippery Sam" had dodged his wartime income tax. Tilden is shown looking in a mirror and saying, "Reform is Necessary Even in S. J. T." Or again the candidate is shown sitting on the lid of a box marked "Tweed," who was then at large, and holding in his hand "The Reform Fan that Blows Hot and Cold" (No. 98). A sign on the wall back of Tilden offers a reward to those who cannot find Tweed, for Nast believed Tilden had allowed the Boss to escape. In any event, connecting Tweed to Tilden would damage the chances of a candidate of reform. Possibly Nast was touched with a little of the "anything to beat Tilden" approach.

It should be added, Nast never accorded individuals, with the exception of Grant, immunity from his attacks because of past favors or party affiliation: Tilden was not excused from other failures because he opposed Tweed; although Sum-

ner was the Senate leader of the Radical opposition to Johnson, Nast turned against him in the 1872 election; Conklin, the head of the Republican faction that sought to run Grant for a third term, was ridiculed by Nast; and Carl Schurz, also a Radical leader, later was scourged by Nast. For a time he relied heavily on the Republican party allegiance as the standard for judging men. In the late seventies, however, he was to break for a long time with Hayes and in 1884 turned his former standards around by rejecting the party because of Blaine's nomination.

When Rutherford B. Hayes became the Republican candidate, Nast was pleased. He had predicted in a cartoon before the convention that the ticket would be Hamilton Fish and Hayes. His first drawing after the convention, "Why We Laugh" (No. 99), showed Nast's pleasure in having predicted fifty percent of the ticket. Hayes as a Union General and a sound money man appealed to the cartoonist's ideas of sound government. Typical of his artistic treatment of Hayes was "Struck—at Sea" (No. 100), showing him as a towering iceberg wrecking the Democratic ship. The anti-Catholic theme was used in many drawings (No. 101).

Vying with the election for public attention was the great Centennial Exposition of 1876. Under the spell of this national birthday party a conscious effort was made by political parties to emphasize unity and forget the division of war. Hayes promised in many campaign speeches to restore the South to civilian rule.

This expression of goodwill Nast refused to endorse. His view of the Centennial had been made clear a year earlier in "The Republic in Danger" (No. 102). Here a giant American eagle holds the serpent of rebellion and slavery in his talons. This spirit of reunion he ridiculed in drawings showing the Democratic tiger and the Republican lamb lying down together. He ran up the Bloody Shirt to the top of his standard and assailed the South as he had done in the past. The two-page drawing showing a paroled Confederate officer sighting a heavy cannon at a ship marked "Constitution and Union" (No. 103) made clear Nast's opposition to a recent Congressional bill to grant amnesty to seven hundred secession leaders who remained unpardoned. Even more effective was cartoon No. 104 depicting the Democratic tiger pulling its tail off in its determination to devour the Republican lamb. Nast's guiding rule of "vote as you shot" governed his drawing No. 105 showing the Democrats as a very hungry wolf and is evident in his continued use of the tiger (No 106) as the symbol for the still rebellious and dangerous Democratic party.

The Democratic party's straddle on the issue of inflation was cleverly ridiculed in a series of drawings of the tiger with two heads. One head is Tilden who was for hard money, and the other head is that of his running mate Hendricks who advocated inflation (Nos. 107, 108). Nast had begun to use the elephant to symbolize the Republican party. He shows it in one cartoon trampling the tiger (No. 109).

The Union was in even more danger than Nast imagined when he drew his campaign pictures. Neither Tilden nor Hayes won a clear electoral majority because returns from three Southern States and Oregon remained in doubt. A long and difficult period lay ahead. Nast drew himself sharpening his pencil and getting ready for work in "No Rest for the Wicked-Sentenced to More Hard Labor" (No. 110). He continued to hammer away at Tilden in "The Best of Friends Must Part" (No. 111) in company with Tammany and Tweed—an association that he had harped on throughout the campaign. Threats of violence and rumors of disaster filled the air. Hotheads shouted "on to Washington" and "Minute Men" began to prepare to march. Amid threats of insurrection, party leaders in Congress decided to appoint a commission of fifteen members to decide the winner. Still it was by no means certain that the commission's decision would be accepted. A Democratic filibuster in Congress to forestall enacting an unfavorable decision was reportedly averted at a meeting in the Wormley Hotel at which Republicans placated Southerners with the promise to withdraw federal troops from Louisiana and South Carolina. Actually, Hayes had made this pledge part of his campaign. Recent scholarship has pointed to an earlier back scenes compromise in which Hayes gained agreement from the Democratic majority in the House of Representatives to elect a Republican as speaker in exchange for his pledge to give Southern representation in the Cabinet

local control of political patronage and federal subsidies for Southern railroads. In any event the commission's strictly partisan 8 to 7 vote upholding the Republican returns from each state was not contested. Hayes officially became President-elect just three days before the inauguration was scheduled.

Hayes, like Lincoln and Grant before him, called Nast's campaign effort "the most powerful single-handed aid we had." Students of the election may doubt the accuracy of this statement in view of the open spending by "visiting statesmen" to win votes in the critical states and rumors of political bargains struck to bring Hayes to the White House. Nevertheless, a grateful Republican party thought enough of Nast's efforts to seek, through the agency of Senator Chandler, to reward him for his honest efforts with $10,000. As on similar occasions the cartoonist refused saying that he had already been paid for his work by Harper's.

In each presidential election since 1864 Nast's work had been an acknowledged force in the success of the winning candidate. Following his own convictions in the choice of a candidate, he had been satisfied by his man's performance as a President. Even the storm of scandal that broke around Grant did not in the least degree lessen the cartoonist's admiration for the General. The Hayes administration, however, proved to be quite a different story.

Originally for Hayes, one of his first supporters for the nomination, and a devoted worker in his campaign, Nast broke with the new President almost as soon as he took office. He did approve of the President's civil service policy as compared to the Democrat's record he depicted in cartoon No. 112 showing Andrew Jackson astride a hog rather than his more customary steed. Although Hayes campaigned for "permanent pacification" of the South, one of his first acts ended military reconstruction, giving form to the spirit of conciliation born of the Centennial. This announcement appalled Nast, an intense patriot and an unreconstructed Unionist, who revered Lincoln and Grant as protectors of the Union. Nast, who knew little about the South, at firsthand, never admired anything Southern. When he warned the nation in 1877 of the probability of renewed rebellion, he was absolutely sincere. To him it was unthinkable that with a bloody war ended only twelve years earlier the rebels could be safely welcomed back into the nation. Many vindictive Republicans shared this opinion. Probably Nast accepted the rumor that the price of the presidency was restoring home rule. Whatever his reasons, the cartoonist as a man of individual opinions and action for the first time in fifteen years was unable to support the Republican administration in power.

Having to abandon his party was the first of a swift series of personal disasters. The editors of *Harper's* created a crisis for Nast by remaining loyal to the Republican ticket they had supported in the campaign. In the past Nast, at such times, turned to Fletcher Harper, the strong friend and defender, who had always seen to it that he had a free hand, but at this point Fletcher died. In the space of a few days Nast had lost his party, paper, and friend—mainstays during all of his career.

Any possible doubt as to the seriousness of his dilemma was at once dispelled. Curtis, with whom he had tangled on several occasions, was an especially ardent champion of civil service and of Hayes and employed the full scope of the editorial pages of *Harper's* to support the President. Nast soon felt pressure to bring his opinions into harmony with those of the editor. Even though he no longer had Fletcher's support, Nast did not yield.

For several months he sought to find his way out of his dilemma by drawing few pictures, none relating to the administration. But his silence, in contrast to the strong editorial support his paper gave Hayes and Nast's own unenthusiastic support, was inevitably interpreted as censure. Letters poured in demanding that Nast express his opinion of the administration. Delay would no longer suffice; something had to be done. During this time Senator Roscoe Conkling, who opposed civil service reform, and Hayes struck at Curtis with the remark that *Harper's* owed all of its fame to Nast. The truth in this assertion was enough to hurt. Shortly a meeting was called at *Harper's*, a stormy session in which the editors argued with Nast that Hayes meant well and must be given every chance to prove himself. Nast agreed finally not to make critical drawings of the President. But the rebellious artist was not yet in a tractable mood; a few days later he drew an exact illustration of the dilemma at *Harper's*. Uncle Sam is shown pushing

Nast down into a chair and saying: "Our Artist must keep cool,, and sit down, and see how it works" (No. 113). When he saw the drawing, Curtis, very much displeased, asked if he were the model for the figure of Uncle Sam pushing Nast down and choking him. Nast saw no humor in this question. The figure of Uncle Sam, he explained testily, represented policy. "Policy," added Nast with prophetic insight, "always strangles individuals."

The trials of 1877 reached a climax for Nast with *Harper's* refusal in July to publish one of his cartoons. Curtis again was the storm center of an incident almost ending Nast's association with the "Journal of Civilization." Holding to his theory that honorable people should never be made the butt of the cartoonist's ire, Curtis took offense at a satirical but unimportant drawing of poet James Russell Lowell. To make matters worse, the drawing was completed, approved, and set up in page proof before Curtis ordered it withdrawn. Nast, unaccustomed to such treatment, was so outraged that he quit *Harper's* altogether for four months. Heretofore he had always enjoyed the security of knowing that his work, whatever its aim, would be accepted. Now, as one of his friends wrote him, his hand would thereafter be paralyzed by uncertainty of acceptance.

In a real sense Nast himself had written the epitaph for a dead era, the era of his freest and greatest work, with his epigram: "Policy always strangles individuals." It was especially true of Nast but to a degree for all journalists. Staffs became larger and editorial policy less personal; profits rather than policies tended to become the first consideration. Much of the remainder of Nast's career was to be spent in trying vainly to recapture the almost ideal conditions under which he had risen to fame. In his quest he began to dream of regaining his independence by establishing his own journal. But those days, like lost youth, were not to return. Nast could not change to meet the taste of a less challenging new epoch. Issues were still vital, but they were no longer violent. The tariff and civil service could not raise the intense partisan feelings of war, Reconstruction, and the drive against Tweed. Then Nast could define issues and attack with the mace rather than with the rapier. His position was clear, his comment always unclouded, and a vast, sympathetic public applauded. Presidential elections had been for him the latest expression of an ageless struggle of right against wrong, wisdom against error. Always his best work bore the stamp of an "intense expression of moral conviction . . . of a flaming sense of righteousness."

With Hayes' inauguration, political and military reconstruction came to an end. To a lesser degree there was a psychological change as well. If Americans still did not agree on the merits of the Union compared to the Confederacy, they devoted less time to the problem. In the new mood of the late 1870's and early 1880's the "Bloody Shirt" was still present, but henceforth it would flap rather than wave. The keenly partisan attitude on public questions that helped Nast so much in his early career was now giving way to apathy. The press in general was becoming politically independent and would signal its final break in 1884. The vast industrial expansion of the day absorbed the attention, interest, and energy of the people. The nation watched Rockefeller and Carnegie build their vast monopolies and reap their rich harvest for a time with admiration but later with growing bitterness toward the malefactors of great wealth. The next American crusade would be a fight to curb the money power. Nast, conservative by nature and well off financially, never stirred to the bugle call of Populist reformers.

Furthermore, while Nast was floundering the changing public temper was matched to perfection by Joseph Keppler who founded a comic paper, a new journalistic form in the United States, called *Puck*, that favored the Democrats; *Judge*, another new comic paper, supported the Republicans. Hence Nast, who once held the field almost alone, now had formidable rivals and journals. It is little wonder that with Fletcher Harper's death and Keppler's immediate success as artist and journal owner, Nast wanted more and more to launch out on his own. But it was at this point that he began losing his public appeal. It was not so much a case of Nast's decline as it was the ascent of his many new rivals.

Harper's, too, was moving in its editorial policy toward entertainment and away from straight news and politics. The forum that had been provided Nast at the very outset of his career was now being withdrawn. His work would have gone well in a daily newspaper, but it was 1896 before dailies began using cartoons on a large scale. It is not clear why Nast did not at least join the new trend in technique, for he was a capable artist. It would appear that he had too much pride either to adopt his rivals' artistic technique of tinted lithographs or their approach. If he made any effort to change, it is not evident in his work.

To Nast the idea was always more important than the presentation. The great day of the editor had passed by 1880. The great "personal journalists," Horace Greeley, James Gordon Bennett, Henry J. Raymond and William Cullen Bryant, were dead, along with their vogue. Reporters now moved to the fore as public interest shifted away from the editorial page to the front page, from opinion to news. In the news, politics became less interesting than the "human interest" story. Newspapers increased in numbers and in circulation, becoming in the process corporations, impersonal and highly organized, like those in industry. Nationwide services and newspaper chains were organized; standardization set in. Group uniformity rather than individual expression became the rule. *Harper's* hold on the public, once supreme in terms of circulation, was directly challenged in the 1880's by *Ladies Home Journal, McClure's Magazine, Munsey's Magazine,* and others. Circulation of some of these reached a figure ten times as great as *Harper's*. The commercial aspect was stressed more than the ideal. As editor William Allen White said of Frank Munsey, he "had about converted a once noble profession into a six per cent investment."

Despite this inexorable trend Nast persisted in thinking that individual journalism might yet be restored. He hoped to get away from profit making entirely by endowing a journal so that public and editorial pressure could be eliminated, and he and all other contributors could express themselves with complete freedom. Who would provide the endowment? A public that had once waited eagerly for Nast's comments was now only mildly interested. The times passed him by. There were to be some great moments left to this man who had known many triumphs. "But the noontide of his glory had slipped by—the sun was already dropping down in the West" as A. B. Paine expressed it in the rounded phrases of the turn of the century rhetoric.

Although the sun of his career was sinking, Nast, feeling he was better equipped than ever for his work, was not aware of it. *Harper's*, despite editorial disagreements, still clamored for his services as did many rival papers. Offers of new lecture tours, including one from Mark Twain, promised financial rewards. He turned them all down. The prospects for his future in cartooning seemed unlimited. He did not need money, for his salary was high, his investments sound, and he owned a beautiful home.

By the end of the fateful year of 1877 even the Hayes administration had not proved to be as hopeless as Nast had feared. The Southern policy was irritating, but Hayes was a sound money man and on this issue the cartoonist could agree sincerely with both his President and his editors. Outstanding among cartoons on this topic was one showing Uncle Sam putting his foot into a trap—inflation through coining silver—made by the face of Senator Stanley Matthews who introduced a bill to remonitize silver (No. 114). Nast made a number of variations on this theme in the next few months. One of the most sarcastic of these was "The Two Georges" (No. 115). From a portrait, George III and George Washington look down on a very seedy Uncle Sam, his foot caught in the Matthews inflation trap. George III suggests that Washington issue a new Farewell Address to bring the present generation up to honest standards of honest money. Except for Nast's increasing inclination to cover his drawing with captions to the detriment of the artistic impact, this is an excellent cartoon.

Inflation seemed a promising subject, but it did not turn out well. Nast was attacked through satirical cartoons in the *Daily Graphic*, whose offers of employment he had refused. They also reprinted some of his 1873 cartoons when he had favored free coinage of silver in contrast to his position in 1878. To Nast's further discomfort, the "free silver" forces in Congress apparently won the battle for inflation with the passage of the Bland-Allison Bill of 1878 requiring the Federal government to purchase and mint a minimum of 2,000,000 ounces of silver each year. Actually, the government employed the bill so as not to bring about

inflation feared at the time of its passage. Nevertheless, the *Graphic* rejoiced in this defeat of "the pencil of Nast."

The artist touched on a variety of problems in his drawings of the late 1870's. As his success at home faltered he tended to become more interested in foreign affairs. The partition of Turkey was the subject of many cartoons and "Taking a Rest (?)—Die Wacht Am—Bismark" (No. 116) is an excellent example of his comments on foreign affairs. Had there been a greater public interest in European politics, he might have done well with drawings on this subject. His flare for making statesmen look ridiculous did not stop at the water's edge.

There was much interest, particularly on the west coast, in Chinese immigration. Under the threats of the radical Workingmen's party, led by the legendary Dennis Kearney, a new California constitution was drafted and approved which was hostile to capitalists and Chinese. Earlier Nast had seen dangers in Chinese immigration. Now he attacked Kearney, doubtless delighted he was Irish, as communistic and anarchistic in "Social Science Solved" (No. 117). The cry of Kearney's followers for a Chinese Exclusion Act reached Congress in 1879 where, despite contrary provisions of the Burlingame Treaty of 1868, a bill was passed forbidding any ship for a ten year period to bring more than fifteen Chinese to the United States on one trip. Nast decried this measure in "A Matter of Taste" (No. 118) even though this stand allied him with President Hayes who vetoed the bill. The artist in this same drawing also attacked James G. Blaine, shown eating a mess of pottage at a table reserved for presidential candidates in the Kearney Restaurant. Later he used this issue against the Plumed Knight during the 1884 presidential race.

Despite problems, fortune seemed to have smiled on Nast in 1878 with the return to the news of his old adversary, Tilden. *The New York Tribune* published a long series of articles purporting to show his connection with corruption and bribes in the Southern states during the months while the disputed election of 1876 was still undecided. Coded letters were uncovered indicating that Tilden had tried to buy votes in 1876 offering $50,000 for Florida, $80,000 for South Carolina, and $5,000 for one Oregon elector. His suspicions of the former New York governor confirmed, Nast depicted Tilden in the "Cipher Mumm(er)y Case" (No. 119).

Furthermore, the wisdom of Hayes' policy of peace and reunion was challenged. Fear replaced trust: Nast caught the mood in "The Millennium—the Tiger and the Lamb Lie Together" (No. 120). In this companion to his prophetic campaign drawing of a year earlier (No. 106), the tiger is alone with a sign around his neck reading "For Republican Lamb Inquire Within." It was such devastatingly clear presentations of elemental issues that marked all of his best work. To cap what for the moment at least seemed a triumph, Nast also drew a sequel to his picture of a year earlier which showed Uncle Sam pushing him down into a chair to wait until the administration had a chance to act. This time Uncle Sam is shown running out the door; Nast is falling through the bottom of the chair (No. 121). As he goes through, he holds aloft the traditional symbol of journalistic defiance—the "scissors." There was no question about printing this cartoon. Curtis had to bow once more as Nast gleefully lampooned the conciliatory policy he had always mistrusted.

Another omen of good fortune was the recognition accorded Nast in 1879 by the nation's military forces. For years he satirized the policy of low peace-time military budgets, frequently using a skeleton to depict the Army or the Navy. In another especially biting comment in cartoon No. 122, he has Uncle Sam, military budget in hand, riding on Congress which was represented by a snail. He failed to revise the nation's fiscal policies, but his efforts won respect, admiration, and gratitude from soldiers and sailors. In an unprecedented move, military units, by subscriptions limited to a quarter, raised enough to purchase Nast a large silver vase shaped like an army canteen and engraved with a drawing of the nation, represented by Columbia, awarding him a medal. The reverse side bore the information that 3,500 officers and enlisted men of the Army and Navy had contributed to the gift.

The sun of his success seemed to have declined slightly if at all by 1880. Nast did indicate occasionally in his drawings some of the difficulty he was experiencing in finding subjects for his pen. Humor had always been a by-product, not the aim

of his work, but in one drawing of this period Nast is surrounded by bad news trying to think of something amusing to draw. He never succeeded. However, the forty-year-old artist, who had married in 1862 with $1.50 in cash and $350 in debts, now possessed an estate estimated at $125,000. *Harper's* did not agree with all his ideas, yet the management knew his value and still paid him a retainer of $5,000 plus a fee for each picture. Indeed, his total income for 1879 was about $25,000 which was the highest he had ever made. Demands on his time and talent were far greater than he could possibly meet.

Nevertheless, the nomination and election of 1880 presented Nast with a series of unpleasant choices. Grant, who had said that he would never accept a third term unless a national crisis made further service to his country a clear duty, allowed his name to be placed in nomination. Although even the General's strongest backers could not see a crisis in 1880, they found other reasons to support him. Nast was embarrassed; he had denounced charges of Caesarism and the third term when *The New York Tribune* raised them some seven years earlier. Swallowing his pride, the cartoonist remained loyal to Grant while not supporting the old hero's campaign. For thirty-five ballots Grant led Blaine by too small a margin to break the deadlock. The third term bid failure spared Nast a great deal of anguish. Yet even for Nast elections were not as exciting as they had once been, and he seems bored with the whole thing in "Our Republic . . ." (No. 123).

His troubles had not ended. As fate would have it, the successful candidate at the Republican convention, James A. Garfield, had in earlier years run afoul of Nast's pencil. In one of his faint rebukes of Grant's administration Nast had condemned the Credit Mobilier railroad scandal and prominently featured among the culprits Garfield, who was alleged to have got $329 out of the $20,000,000 stolen. (In drawing No. 87 the figure second from the left of Justice is Garfield.) A lesser cartoonist might have escaped from this situation unnoticed. Not Nast, for the Democrats had suffered too much at his hand in earlier campaigns to overlook any chance to discredit him and weaken the Republicans. The Nast cartoon of Garfield as a wrongdoer and the incriminating sum

"$329" chalked on walls and fences were prime Democratic propaganda in 1880. Thus by a turn of fate Nast's attacks, weak as they were, on Grant scandals had come back to haunt him.

The developments at the Democratic convention added still more to Nast's woes. His personal friend Winfield Scott Hancock, a former Union general, won the nomination. The unhappy penman was caught between two fires. The Republican party that he deeply revered was supporting a man he disliked and condemned. The Democratic party, still to him best symbolized by the hungry tiger of rebellion, nominated a man he admired and respected. Not a few conferences were held at Frankin Square among the editors of *Harper's* in an attempt to get Nast to support the Republican party. As usual, he was not amenable to direction. At last Nast agreed to support the Republican party while attacking the Democratic party as an organization. For the most part he would ignore the two candidates.

In what for Nast was a gentle vein he showed the General as a Gulliver bound by the little men of his party (No. 124), or as a bewildered platform speaker asking his introducer nervously, "Who is tariff and why is he for revenue only?" Nast attacked the Democratic party and the South with full vigor still waving the Bloody Shirt in "As Solid and Defiant as Ever" (No. 125). Here is shown a menacing Confederate with a KKK cap, a Tammany tiger tail, and slave whip, standing, pistols in hand, on a platform of "The Same Principles We Fought for Four Years." Another presentation of this theme showed Robert Toombs of Georgia, the celebrated unreconstructed rebel, as a giant holding a very small Hancock in one hand. The cartoon was an accurate appraisal of Nast's emphasis on partisan and war issues rather than the personalities and problems of 1880 (No. 126). Even Nast could not arouse much enthusiasm for what had finally become an outworn line.

Nast could find no overpowering issues in the election of 1880 on which to hang his drawings (No. 127, 128, 129), for there were none. The two parties were, in Lord James Bryce's phrase, like two bottles, each stamped with a label and each one empty. Even if he had not chosen to make his campaign impersonal, neither Garfield nor Hancock was a character colorful enough to inspire

any strong public reaction. The voters were as much at a loss as was Nast in choosing between this passive pair, and the final tally showed Garfield with a popular majority of only 7,000 out of more than 9 million votes cast. This election was typical of the cartoonist's problem of popular apathy and neutrality shown by the fact that in the total votes of all the elections from 1872 to 1892 the margin of Republican victory was only 4,000. "During the whole of this period the electorate played a game of blindman's buff. Never before had American politics been so intellectually bankrupt." When these liabilities were compounded by Nast's personal involvement with the two candidates of 1880, his influence was almost neutralized. It was impossible to establish that clear allegiance to right versus wrong that was the basis of effective cartooning.

His bewilderment is shown when despite his partisan campaign cartoons he celebrated Garfield's inauguration by having North and South walk hand in hand led by industry into a peaceful future (No. 130). Possibly his most effective cartoon was No. 131. It shows a working man looking at an empty dinner pail, represented as one of the changes brought about by the Democrats who had made "Change" their campaign slogan. Here Nast caught the mood of the times. Yet, for the man who had fought the spiritual evils of rebellion and civic corruption with thunderous denunciations, the turn of a presidential election on the possibility of an empty dinner pail was spiritually lacking. It was appealing to voters, however. Possibly this unheroic symbol was one of his more important contributions to his party. In any event "Four more years of the full dinner pail" was the clarion call that thrilled the ardent supporters of McKinley twenty years later.

After the election Nast was concerned by Garfield's inability to reconcile powerful factions in the Republican party. Roscoe Conkling, the leader of the Stalwart faction, had failed in his effort to put Grant on the ticket. The Half-Breeds, so called because they were half stalwart and half reformer, as a concession agreed to allow his close henchman, Chester A. Arthur, to be the Vice Presidential nominee. Conkling supported the ticket and helped hold several doubtful states for Garfield. Conkling, overvaluing his contributions, expected as a reward nothing less than virtual control of the administration. He was rebuffed and then humiliated when Garfield selected his greatest party rival, James G. Blaine, leader of the rival Half-Breed faction, as Secretary of State. Furious, Conkling soon resigned from the Senate and returned to New York to seek re-election as a vote of confidence. Nast stood with Garfield and ridiculed Conkling (Nos. 132, 133). The New Yorker, having definitely overplayed his hand, was defeated. These events helped bring Nast back to support both President and party. The cartoonist's reconciliation was complete when the shock of Garfield's assassination forged unity and restored Nast, after a number of trials, to peace with his party.

He was not, however, at peace with his world. In 1880 a new method of reproduction for pictures was instituted at *Harper's*. Drawings were now made in ink on paper and reproduced by a photo-chemical process. The new process constituted a major change in technique, for throughout his career Nast had drawn with soft pencil on box-wood blocks which were then hand engraved. Many of the small blocks he cut himself. Few men mastered their medium as he did. He never adjusted completely to the new method with the virtuosity that marked the old. His pen line tended to be thin and delicate rather than heavy and direct as in his pencil drawings. Part of this change was artistic development toward an economy of means and the 1884 campaign against Blaine was well drawn. Later drawings in the 1880's seem faded and weak as compared to the boldly assured line that was once his trade mark. Purpose as well as technique may have been at fault. Perhaps it was only coincidence, yet the light and timid line seems to mirror a man less confident and certain of the unalterable rightness of his convictions and the warmth of their public reception. It was becoming increasingly difficult to find publishers for anything other than semi-critical comment or innocuous observation that marked political cartooning in the hands of most of his contemporaries.

There was, in fact, little work of any sort from Nast's studio during the next three years. The friction between the cartoonist and the Harper brothers continued. As astute businessmen they had altered the journal to suit the changing taste of the public. It had become less a man's paper—a journal of politics and reform—and more a magazine for the whole family, featuring items of social and domestic interest with little place for political broadsides. Finally Nast, who felt financially independent at the moment, wrote one of his infrequent letters to the management of *Harper's*. In it he complained that formerly when his work was not accepted for publication he had been given a reason for the decision. Of late, he continued, much of his work was rejected with no reason given for suppressing it. "Hence, I am forced to the conclusion that for some reason unknown to me, my drawings are no longer of use to you, and that under those circumstances you certainly cannot care to continue the arrangement with me. . . ."

John W. Harper, Jr., then in charge, in an answer that was friendly but firm insisted that no drawing had been turned down without good reason and that Nast himself had failed to allow any opportunity for explanations as to why the work was rejected. The real source of contention Harper made clear by reminding the artist: "You ought to remember that we have to consider these matters from a business standpoint, as well as from their artistic merits." Evidently, this was a fair statement, but Nast did not want to hear why his drawings were unacceptable. He wanted to have all of them accepted as had been the case in Fletcher Harper's day. Although the connection with *Harper's* was not broken off, the next year Nast devoted himself to travel in England and the United States and did not get back into the pages of *Harper's* until March, 1884, when the impending election restored his interest in the political scene. Several times John W. Harper, Jr. had challenged him to come back with an incisive cartoon that would prove to his enemies that his eye was undimmed and that his hand had not lost its cunning. He succeeded in doing this with the drawing, "The Sacred Elephant," his Republican symbol, with the chair of leadership empty upon its back, and Nast himself in the lower corner with the caption, "This animal is sure to win, if it is only kept pure and clean, and has not too heavy a load to carry" (No. 134).

It seemed that a new and happier day was at hand. The illusion did not last long. Restless under his unfavorable working conditions and anxious to amass enough capital to start his own paper, Nast

invested $30,000 in the firm of Grant and Ward, in
which U. S. Grant, Jr. was a partner. This was
considered gilt-edged stock and for a time dividends were generous. When in May, 1884, the
company failed, the whole country was shocked.
For Nast it was both a financial disaster, taking
everything but his home, and a severe disillusion-
ment. Too late he found that the company while
using Grant's name to inspire confidence had been
fraudulent from the start. Ward, it developed, was
highly skilled at taking money out of one drawer
and putting it into another and had used new investors' money to cover dividends to old investors.
There seemed now almost no possibility that Nast
might establish his own paper and reestablish his
lost independence.

Dreams had been shunted aside for the necessity
of earning a living. It was difficult for a man who
had grown accustomed to wealth and leisure to set
himself to adjust to poverty. But Nast was still
comparatively young and his reputation was still
great. In his new stringency it was a blow almost
as shocking as his financial loss to find himself
later in 1884 unable to support the Republican
ticket for President. Nast disliked James G. Blaine,
showing him as early as 1879 in satirical caricatures of his policy on Chinese exclusion (No. 135).
Blaine, nevertheless, was a faithful Republican
with claims on the nomination that could not in-
definitely be ignored.

Harper's editor, George William Curtis, was a
Republican convention delegate and unofficial
leader of the party's liberal reform faction. Despite his best efforts he failed to block Blaine's
path to victory. After the convention Curtis and
the other members of the "Journal of Civilization's"
board of directors repudiated the Republican ticket.
For once, Nast was heartily in favor of his su-
perior's policy. Indeed he declared he would not
support Blaine, even if the Democrats nominated
the Devil.

Few journals and few men had been so closely
identified with Republican success, almost from
the origins of the party, as had *Harper's* and Nast.
Defection was a serious blow to the party. Nast was
pilloried in picture and in print. *Judge* wrote:

Poor, poor T. Nast
Thy day is past—
Thy bolt is shot, thy die is cast—
Thy pencil point
Is out of joint—
Thy pictures lately disappoint.

The cartoons in *Judge* also took Nast to task,
and the great caricaturist found himself frequently
the victim of his own pen. As in 1880, his former
drawings were used against him. The vagaries of
political fortune cast Carl Schurz as Nast's fellow
worker. Opposing journals had no trouble finding
Nast's savage strictures on Schurz for use in opposing Grant in 1872. In the age of personal journalism the major emphasis was on the man. So
a measure of Nast's impact on his times was the
degree to which he became a political issue in the
presidential elections of 1872 through 1884.

Despite unfavorable reactions from party die-
hards, Nast was by no means alone in his opposition
to Blaine. Many Republicans found Blaine, as Nast
so graphically put it, too heavy a load even for
the Republican elephant. In a major revolt, the
Independent Republicans, or Mugwumps, left the
party in a civil war of politics. As brother had
been pitted against brother in 1861, the brother-
hood of Republicans was rent in twain in 1884.

The Democrats passed over the Devil and
trusted their future to Grover Cleveland, former
reform Mayor of Buffalo and Governor of New
York. Nast had a leader he could support. In a
prophetic vein he had drawn Cleveland in 1882
before he became governor as an angel in a
spotless robe having the two "wings" of the
Democratic party fitted to his back. A later drawing showed him taking a flyer for the White House.

Personalities dominated the election of 1884
as in few other contests. Dissensions and disagreements were the breath of life to Nast. The old
warrior was once again in his element in de-
lineating the differences between Grover the Good
and the Plumed Knight. There was ample material
for satire at hand; Blaine's long public career
made him vulnerable to attack. Like a Sampson
whose strength returned for one last glorious effort, Nast drew cartoons filled with the sharp
satire of his great days as with consistent skill he
derided and mocked the "Plumed Knight." Probably only his campaign against Greeley surpassed

the savagery of this effort. Blaine the incarnation of the loyal Republican party was Nast's target and what a magnificent target with his tentative eyes and pseudo dignity of carriage, always appearing very conscious that his picture was being taken. Even the eloquent title which Ingersoll had bestowed upon him in 1876, The Plumed Knight, became an instrument of satire in the cartoonist's hand. Three bedraggled plumes hung limply from Blaine's tall top hat in most of the drawings. Often he was shown as a ridiculous looking knight. The statesman's literary masterpiece, *Twenty Years of the Republic,* was ridiculed in almost every drawing just as Greeley's fondness in his editorials for the phrase, "What I know about . . .," had been so effectively used in 1872. Like Greeley, Blaine was a distinct personality and thus the complete victim of Nast's pen.

"Is this 'The True American Policy'?" (No. 136) asked Nast in the drawing showing Blaine on his knees, not for prayer, as was the case with Washington or Lincoln, but to plead for the Irish vote. Again Blaine was shown as a rhinoceros, the most thick-skinned of animals, fond of wallowing in mud, bearing on his back the celebrated Mulligan letters, evidence of his fraud in using his public office to gain government favors for the Little Rock Railroad and private profit for himself (No. 137). Blaine would have had to be thick-skinned indeed to have ignored Nast's use of the indictment of those letters in No. 138. The Man from Maine was cleverly parodied as a jousting knight trying to win the prize of public money in "The 'Great American' Game of Public Office for Private Gain" (No. 139), as opposed to Cleveland's slogan: "A public office is a public trust." Possibly the sharpest of all Nast's arrows, "The Self-Convicted Knight" (No. 140), again uses the Mulligan Letters. Blaine is shown as "Yesterday" kneeling and with tears in his eyes asking for the return of letters that would impugn

his honor while as "Today" he declares there was nothing in the letters that is not consistent with integrity.

Taken by itself Nast's work was as good as any that he had ever done even though neither candidate was a veteran, and the Bloody Shirt was but a frayed pink shadow of the battle banner of the '60's and '70's. Yet the public was so completely captivated by the drawings of Barnhard Gilliam and Keppler that it paid relatively little heed to the fine work of its former favorite.

Nevertheless, the election of Cleveland, the first Democrat to win since 1856 and the only one Nast sponsored, was for the cartoonist a personal victory in which conscience and principle prevailed over prudence and partisanship. The artist's joy was short-lived, for this success was most costly. His break with the Republican party lost him a number of friends and supporters among its "dyed-in-the- wool" partisans who had always admired his work. These losses were not matched in number by the new friends he won. There could hardly be a place in Democratic hearts for the man who had caused them untold grief over two decades. While his help was gladly accepted, the new union was an alliance of war, not a meeting of minds.

Harper's suffered a great deal also. The management had estimated that abandoning the Republican party would cost $50,000. This proved far too conservative; commercially the "Journal of Civilization" had made a serious mistake.

For Nast the implications of this financial disaster were serious. Battle heat had fused Nast and *Harper's* staff into a unit once more, but when the struggle ended, the unity it had brought soon faded. The management, now more than ever, had to be concerned with profits and could not afford tolerance for an artist who had very decided ideas of his own and was totally oblivious to the practical considerations of business.

6

LAST YEARS

WITH Cleveland's victory in 1884 Nast kept intact his record of supporting the winning candidate in each of six presidential campaigns in which he participated. Rather than a new start the 1884 Blaine series was the cartoonist's last great moment. The yoke of unsympathetic editorship in the early 1880's irked Nast more and more. He lingered on at *Harper's* until the end of 1886, but these last years, with the exception of the few months in 1884, were neither pleasant nor productive. Financial reverses made it necessary for Nast to sell pictures, but for the most part they were mediocre as compared to his own high standard. Only occasional sparks attested to the fire his pen once flashed; the assurance and dash that lent distinction to his best works were rarely evident. For him the times were out of joint. It would have taken a man far more pliant than Nast to support any national Democratic administration or to praise Tammany Hall for a reform program. He had spent too many years condemning them as dangers to the Republic (Nos. 141, 142, 145). Response to his cartoons was apathetic because the public simply was no longer engrossed with politics.

Nevertheless, Nast himself was possessed by the feeling that his pen rather than his public failed him as he attempted to point out the dangers in anarchism (Nos. 143, 144). There was pathos in his use of Boss Tweed, the symbol of his greatest accomplishment, in drawing No. 146. When compared to the original Tweed cartoons they show all too clearly Nast's decline in technique brought on by the passing of wood engraving so suited to his skills. Possibly some men could have adjusted to such rapid changes in methods and moods. Nast could not. Half-hearted, unconvincing work was beneath him. Dissatisfied with himself yet still hoping that he might again capture the smile of fortune in some new surroundings, he ended his

work for *Harper's* with the Christmas drawings for 1886 (Nos. 147, 148). It was appropriate that his last drawings should be on a universal theme transcending the fortunes of politics and the whims of the public. Thus at forty-six the artist ended his twenty-nine years of association with *Harper's*.

Henry Watterson, the famous editor of the *Louisville Courier-Journal*, frequently an opponent but always a Nast admirer, wrote of this historic event, "In quitting *Harper's Weekly*, Nast lost his forum: in losing him, *Harper's Weekly* lost its political importance." As "the pictorial advocate, censor, and statesman of his age he will always remain the prime example of the greatest possible force of political satire."

Harper's, conscious of its loss, sought to hold Nast. He was urged to take a rest, and his retainer was paid for a year with the understanding that he would prepare books of his old Christmas drawings and Tweed Ring cartoons for publication. Only the first of these was completed. Under the title, *Christmas Drawings for the Human Race*, it represents an important facet of Nast's talent and one that gave him great pleasure. Throughout his career he had turned aside from his pressing task, be it saving the Union, prosecuting Tweed, or electing a President, to celebrate Christmas. The best of these drawings are personifications of Santa Claus as striking in a graphic form as "The Night Before Christmas" is in literary form. Much of Nast's contemporary and enduring fame was based on these works (Nos. 149-153).

Succeeding generations of artists have made very few if any alterations in Nast's jolly, bearded, bright-eyed, characterizations of Santa Claus dressed in fur with a sprig of holly in his cap. Indeed, if Santa were suddenly incarnated, he would be declared an impostor if he did not resemble Nast's conception in almost every detail. Just as George Washington is tied in the national mind to Gilbert Stuart, Santa is linked to Thomas Nast. This has proved to be a most important part of his legacy to his country. It is safe to say that not a Christmas goes by without a number of journalistic tributes to the artist as "the man who made Santa Claus." His drawings are frequently borrowed to enliven, with their timeless magic, the pages of yuletide newspapers and invoke the true spirit of Christmas.

Still dreaming of a new journal with the motto, "Principles, not Men," Nast gathered the last of his fast-dwindling financial resources for investment in one more "sure thing." This time it was a mine in the West. As before, his bright hopes were not fulfilled in hard cash. Now times indeed became difficult for the artist. *Harper's* invited him in 1888 to draw cartoons for the presidential election, but he definitely felt he had no place on the "Journal of Civilization" and declined. When he sought work elsewhere, he found to his surprise and dismay that his talent was no longer adequate. A number of journals gave him work. In each case his independence, or perhaps his inability to adjust at this late stage in his career, soon brought a break with the editors. One job after another ended after only a few weeks.

Finally, an assignment with the *New York Gazette* brought his quest of his own paper to fruition. The *Gazette* was doing so poorly it was facing bankruptcy. No new backers could be found. More by default than otherwise he inherited the paper, and at last in 1893 his own paper, *Nast's Weekly*, was launched. It was not, alas, the well endowed journal he had envisioned. In fact, it took another mortgage on his house, his only material possession, to get his paper started. For a time ephemeral hopes of financial assistance from other sources kept the project going. Failure came swiftly when help did not materialize. Bitterly disappointed, the cartoonist saw *Nast's Weekly* follow many another short-lived journal into limbo. With a meager and uncertain income, he found himself buried by thousands of dollars in accumulated debts.

These late years never brought a turning of the road. Almost as painful as his heavy financial burden was the slowly growing suspicion that the public no longer cared for his work. His name and past fame were still venerated, yet the skill once in such

favor no longer stirred public interest. This realization nearly broke his heart. To rise from obscurity to fame had been a fascinating and invigorating experience; to fall from fame to obscurity was a trying and soul-searing one.

Not infrequently he was the subject of feature articles dealing with him as a figure of the past. Letters addressed to *Harper's* often referred to the "late Thomas Nast." Occasionally, he would answer one of these with a letter made up of a small drawing of himself with the words, "I still live." Yet, he himself came to realize that professionally this was not completely so. An idea would strike, and he would complete a sketch, look at it awhile, then comment that no one would publish it. "Tommy Nast, you're dead!" he would say. His work came to an end in 1901 with a Christmas drawing for *Leslie's*, the first journal he had served some forty-six years earlier.

President Theodore Roosevelt, a staunch admirer over the years, received from Nast in 1901 an oil painting of Santa for his children. Early the next year Roosevelt, knowing of Nast's misfortunes, appointed him American consul to Guayaquil, Ecquador. He accepted the job, although he would have much preferred assignment to his native Germany. Jobs were few and the cartoonist was in no position to bargain. When friends asked him why he was going to Guayaquil, he answered that it was to learn how to pronounce the city's name. Good humor and great courage remained with him to the end. That end was not long coming in the tropical climate to which he had been assigned. In 1902 Nast died of yellow fever at the age of sixty-two.

In retrospect, Nast at the height of his career was the acknowledged master of American cartooning. Now almost a century later he is still universally accorded that recognition. In rich abundance he possessed the moral purpose, courage, adherence to truth as he saw it, incisive wit, and high artistic skill that must be the endowment of any successful caricaturist. Certainly no less important was his ability to awaken public interest in his work and influence public attitudes.

Even the greatest actor must have a stage and an audience. For Nast *Harper's Weekly* provided both. His greatest years were likewise *Harper's* greatest. Both the artist and the journal declined at the same time. All of these assets would not have guaranteed fame to Nast. Great cartoonists like great presidents emerge from great crises. While favorable conditions do not assure success, adverse conditions often cause failure. Over the last two centuries American cartooning has flourished best when great political issues and figures held the nation's attention. The ideal situation for the caricaturist is to be against a universally recognized threat that is both powerful and destructive, but not impossible to defeat. In this respect Nast was fortunate in that the Civil War, Reconstruction, and the Tweed Ring gave him perfect opportunities to reach his greatest potential. Only slightly less important to the caricaturist are national figures who are powerful, picturesque, and colorful. Hardly better targets for the cartoonist can be imagined than Greeley, Tweed, Hall, Tilden, Conkling, and Blaine! Nast demonstrated in the latter stages of his own career that even a genius is hard put to overcome perverse fate.

Like the majority of cartoonists Nast was conservative as were the journals on which he worked. The stirring issues of the 1880's, when Nast began to decline, were the beginnings of such Populist reforms as antitrust laws, free silver, national ownership of railroads, and graduated income taxes. Had Nast agreed with these policies he could have drawn effective cartoons against the powerful and menacing status quo. He did not agree. Again he might have continued his success if Populism had reached its peak in the early 1880's. Occasionally he attacked populism, communism, and socialism, but again they did not present the immediate menace of a Tweed or a Andrew Johnson. It was impossible to generate any great enthusiasm in protecting institutions and ideas that appeared to be quite self sufficient. Most cartoonists, including Nast, are better able to deal with politics which revolves around people than with economic issues which are abstract and institutionalized. The Supreme Court might rule that the Standard Oil Company was an individual, but this was not clear enough to the populace to aid the cartoonist.

In the latter years of his life a fickle public tired of his uncompromising condemnations. Tolerance and apathy replaced the militant national mood of partisanship and action. "The public, in its preoccupation with worldly pursuits, asked of its painters only that they present no problems or surprises." The popular painters of the day showed "one common denominator: a safe and sober mediocrity that could be admired without effort." The nation in the 1880's and 1890's became more self satisfied, more preoccupied with profits, and less concerned with policy. There simply was a dearth of pictorial topics. Even a Paul Revere could not stir continued excitement had he ridden on a regular schedule every night. "The world," violinist Fritz Kreisler once explained, "is a great child and tires easily. You cannot make friends for long with the world." It was not strange that Thomas Nast's world tired of him; rather his mastery over it for so long a time was remarkable and all the more so when it is remembered that mass circulation of magazines and daily newspaper cartoons were phenomena of the 1890's. Nast had the more difficult task of stirring the best people—the good but satisfied people of means and position whose crusading spirit died in the 1870's.

Satirists, it is said, seldom end well. The rage that fills them touches other men only slightly. For a time conditions may make the public share the satirist's indignation, but such times are short. In an era that demanded heavy-handed ridicule Nast was a master. An unreasonable man, however, he tried to shape the world to his own standards. Reasonable men tend to accept the world as it is. Only for awhile did they sympathize with him. In the new age that demanded nothing more than amusement, he was doomed to be a misfit and a failure. Yet few men enjoy fame, let alone twenty-five years of it. For Nast fame came early, and obscurity covered the middle and late years that might have been normally the more productive ones. Once he was called a poet of pictures, and poets, not uncommonly, burn out their genius early.

He was not, however, a poet of universal appeal. Few of his pictures escape confines of time, place, and person to reach the higher plane of universal symbols as did so many of the satires of the great masters of social criticism such as England's William Hogarth or the incomparable Henri Daumier of France. The intimate immediacy Nast thus gained by identifying his work with the happenings of the moment increased his jouralistic effectiveness; indeed, it was indispensable although costly to its lasting artistic value. Nor do Nast's works, in the main, exhibit irony, skepticism, and pessimism, the usual elements of great satire. He had no attitude of wistful sorrow arising from disappointment at understandable human failing. His attack was somewhat harsh moral condemnation based on contempt for unpardonable sin. Satire he achieved, although great satire of universal appeal was not possible within the limits of nineteenth century journalism. It has eluded many other American cartoonists and painters. The partisan could appreciate the appeal of a sharp cartoon that stung his enemy. But there was not in American culture the maturity, the wisdom, the tragedy that in Old World countries created an appreciation for the subtle art of satirizing the humdrum frauds of everyday society. Nast was able in his early years to meet almost the only widespread demand for art work that existed in the United States—an adjunct to partisan, personal journalism, rather than an expression of appreciation for caricature as an end in itself.

In the general development of American art as distinct from cartooning and caricature Nast's contribution has been significant. His work was practical with artistic problems of composition, line, light, and shadow important only to the degree that they fostered the cartoonist's major purpose of presenting an idea. His concentration on American institutions, intense interest in society, and unflagging, although not revolutionary, zeal for reform in some measure found their way into the realm of fine art through the social protest in this century of men like John Sloan, George Bellows, Fletcher Martin, and William Gropper. The turn of the century "Ash Can School" of artistic realism reflected a social consciousness that reported conditions in American life exactly as they were. Nast reported conditions as they were in the hope of changing them to what he felt they should become.

A more important and direct contribution to art was Nast's ability to command attention and build up a wide audience. Americans who ignored pictures before Nast's day were awakened to the existence of and practical value of graphic art. An incalculable service was rendered in showing Americans that their own people could express themselves in art. Popular aesthetic horizons were expanded.

It is said that Nast was too original to have founded a school of cartooning. This is true in matters of technique and style of presentation. What has been utilized from his work are the ideas and the aims. Few political cartoonists have equaled his comic presentation of serious subjects. Indeed, today the process has been reversed and comic artists such as Al Capp or Walt Kelley have lent political overtones to their essentially comic presentations.

In short, Nast was what he sought to be, a great editorial cartoonist, a master of what is perhaps the most difficult journalistic form. With only a few strokes of a pen he had to make so significant a comment on the news that the casual reader could understand it at a glance. This he was able to do not on a few special occasions but with remarkable consistency week after week over a period of two decades. "Journalism," it has been well said, "is the criticism of the moment at the moment and caricature is that criticism at once simplified and intensified by a plastic form." Thomas Nast was never content to confine himself to report events or to reflect the philosophy of his editors when it clashed with his own. An impassioned participant he sought rather to direct events in accordance with his own ideas through his immense influence on public opinion. Perhaps no one ever succeeded as well in achieving this purpose. "The list of cartoonists who have influenced public opinion begins with Thomas Nast, and he still leads all later men in both power and the breadth of his appeal," wrote William Murrell in *A History of American Graphic Humor*. At the crest of his career Nast was "an American oracle obliquely speaking wisdom in humorous symbols, riddles, and parables."

BIBLIOGRAPHY

Becker, Stephen, *Comic Art in America*. New York: Simon and Schuster, 1959

Bigelow, John, *Life of Samuel J. Tilden*. New York: Harper and Brothers, 1895

"Bill Mauldin: 'Hit it if its big,' " *Time* (July 21, 1961), pp. 50-54

Bishop, Joseph B., "Early Political Caricature in America," *Century* (June, 1892), pp. 219-231

Bowen, Croswell, *The Elegant Oakey*. New York: Oxford University Press, 1956

Breen, Matthew P., *Thirty Years of New York Politics*. New York: No publisher listed, 1899

Callow, Alexander B., *The Tweed Ring*. New York: Oxford University Press, 1966

Craven, Thomas, ed., *Cartoon Cavalcade*. New York: Simon and Schuster, 1943

Davis, Elmer, *History of the New York Times, 1851-1920*. New York: The New York Times, 1921

DuBois, G. P., "Thomas Nast," *Arts Weekly* (March, 1932), p. 28

Gutman, W., "American Phenomenon," *Creative Art*, Vol. 5, pp. 670-672

Harper, John H., *The House of Harper*. New York: Harper Brothers, 1912

Lorant, Stefan, *Lincoln: A Picture Story of His Life*. New York: Harper, 1957

Lynch, Denis Tilden, *"Boss" Tweed: The Story of a Grim Generation*. New York: Boni and Liveright, 1927

Matchet, J., "Art of Caricature and Cartooning," *Design* (December, 1936), p. 35

Mauldin, Bill, *What's Got Your Back Up?* New York: Harper, 1962

Mitchell, J. A., "Contemporary Caricature," *Scribner's* (December, 1889), pp. 120-129

Mott, Frank Luther, *American Journalism: A History, 1690-1960*. 3rd ed. New York: The Macmillan Company, 1962

Murrell, William, *A History of American Graphic Humor, 1865-1938*. New York: The Macmillan Company, 1938

Myers, Gustavus, *The History of Tammany Hall*. New York: By the author, 1901

Nast, Thomas, *Christmas Drawings for the Human Race*. New York: Harper and Brothers, 1889

"Nast Phillippics Against Tammany in 1871 Seem Topical Today," *Art Digest* (October, 1935), p. 21

Nevins, Allan and Frank Weitenkampf, *A Century of Political Cartoons: Caricature in the United States from 1800-1900*. New York: Charles Scribner's Sons, 1944

Oberholtzer, E. P., *A History of the United States Since the Civil War*. New York: The Macmillan Company, 1928

Paine, Albert Bigelow, *Th. Nast: His Period and His Pictures*. New York: Harper and Brothers, 1904

————————, "Harper's Weekly and Thomas Nast," *Harper's Weekly* (January 5, 1907), pp. 14-18

————————, "Origin of American Cartoon Symbols," *Harper's Weekly* (September 19, 1908), pp. 11-12

Price, Richard G. G., *A History of Punch*. London: Collins, 1957

"Roly Poly," *Time* (March 21, 1932), pp. 41-42

Schooling, John Holt, "England and America, as Illustrated by 'Punch,' " *The Strand Magazine* (May, 1903), pp. 431-437

Stuart, Sylvia, "Political Cartoons," *Hobbies* (October, 1936), pp. 8-9

"Thomas Nast," *Harper's Weekly* (December 10, 1865), p. 339

"Thomas Nast," *Harper's Weekly* (May 11, 1867), pp. 293-294

Thomas Nast, the Man Who Made Santa Claus. New York: The Marchbanks Press, 1958

Vinson, J. Chal, "Thomas Nast and the American Political Scene," *American Quarterly* (Fall, 1957), pp. 337-344

Werner, M. R., *Tammany Hall*. New York: Doubleday, Doran, 1928

INDEX

*Numbers in parentheses refer to illustrations.

43

ILLUSTRATIONS

E PRESENTATION OF THE CHINESE AMBASSADOR.

1

REFLECTION.

2

"FAREWELL, A LONG FAREWELL, TO ALL MY GREATNESS."—*King Henry VIII.*

LINCOLN'S TWO DIFFICULTIES.

3

LIN "WHAT! NO MONEY! NO MEN!"

"BEECHER'S AMERICAN SOOTHING SYRUP."

4

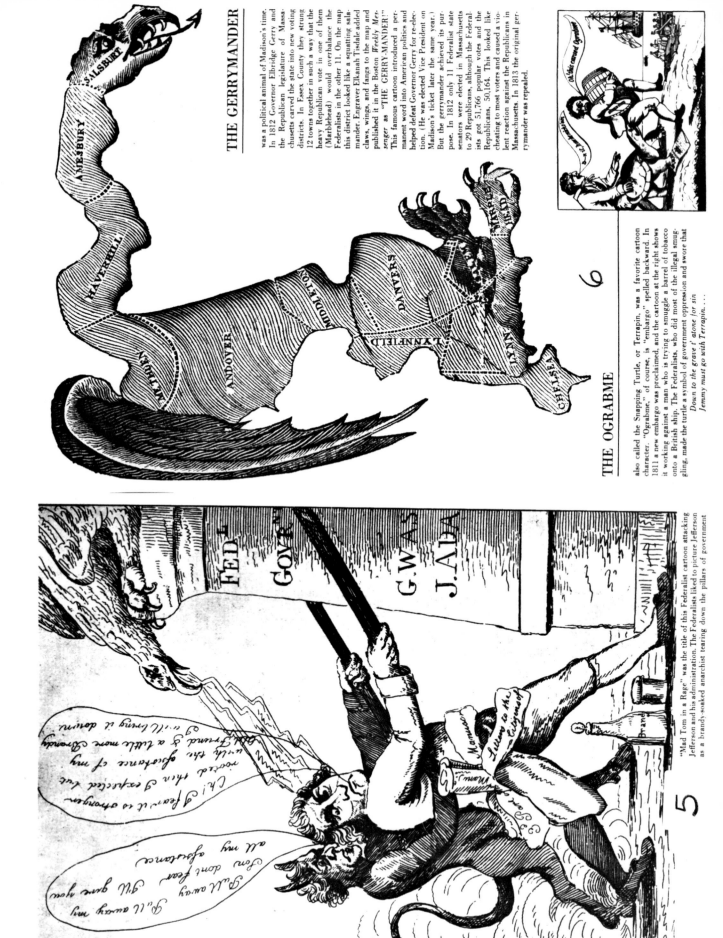

THE GERRYMANDER

was a political animal of Madison's time. In 1812 Governor Elbridge Gerry and the Republican legislature of Massachusetts carved the state into new voting districts. In Essex County they strung 12 towns together in such a way that the heavy Republican vote in one of them (Marblehead) would overbalance the Federalists in the other 11. On the map this district looked like a squatting salamander. Engraver Elkanah Tisdale added claws, wings, and fangs to the map and published it in the Boston *Weekly Messenger* as "THE GERRY-MANDER." This famous cartoon introduced a permanent word into American politics and helped defeat Governor Gerry for re-election. (He was elected Vice President on Madison's ticket later the same year.) But the gerrymander achieved its purpose. In 1812 only 11 Federalist state senators were elected in Massachusetts to 29 Republicans, although the Federalists got 51,766 popular votes and the Republicans, 50,164. This looked like cheating to most voters and caused a violent reaction against the Republicans in Massachusetts. In 1813 the original gerrymander was repealed.

6

THE OGRABME

also called the Snapping Turtle, or Terrapin, was a favorite cartoon character. "Ograbme," of course, is "embargo" spelled backward. In 1811 a new embargo was proclaimed, and the cartoon at the right shows it working against a man who is trying to smuggle a barrel of tobacco onto a British ship. The Federalists, who did most of the illegal smuggling, made the turtle a symbol of government oppression and swore that

Down to the grave I' alone for sin
Jemmy must go with Terrapin. . . .

5

"Mad Tom in a Rage" was the title of this Federalist cartoon attacking Jefferson and his administration. The Federalists liked to picture Jefferson as a brandy-soaked anarchist tearing down the pillars of government

"The Doctors Puzzled" shows Mother Bank disgorging the Government's funds into smaller banks. Biddle sits on her neck, while Clay, Webster, and Calhoun consult on the sad case. Jackson and Downing peek through the window.

"Political Quixotism" shows Jackson as the victim of an anti-Bank nightmare. Downing, representing the public, tries to haul him back to bed by his suspenders. This cartoon appeared when people were tired of the Bank war.

HARPER'S WEEKLY.

JOURNAL OF CIVILIZATION.

Vol. VI.—No 299.]   NEW YORK, SATURDAY, SEPTEMBER 20, 1862.   [SINGLE COPIES SIX CENTS.
$2 50 PER YEAR IN ADVANCE.

Entered according to Act of Congress, in the Year 1862, by Harper & Brothers, in the Clerk's Office of the District Court for the Southern District of New York.

A GALLANT COLOR-BEARER.—[SEE NEXT PAGE.]

CHRISTMAS EVE, 1862

THE RESULT OF WAR—VIRGINIA IN 1863

THE BATTLE OF FREDERICKSBURG

THANKSGIVING - DAY.

THE UNION ALTAR.

14

THANKSGIVING-DAY, NOVEMBER 26, 1863.

COMPROMISE WITH THE SOUTH.

DEDICATED TO THE CHICAGO CONVENTION.

ELECTION-DAY,
8TH NOVEMBER.

NO COMPROMISE.

THE VETERAN'S VOTE.

16

TO MY COUNTRY FOR WHICH I HAVE FOUGHT AND DIED . . . A CURSE UPON YOU, FOR MAKING ME APPEAR DISLOYAL.

HOW THE COPPERHEADS OBTAIN THEIR VOTES.—[See First Page.]

TIMELY WARNING,

TO UNION MEN.

THE NEW ORLEANS

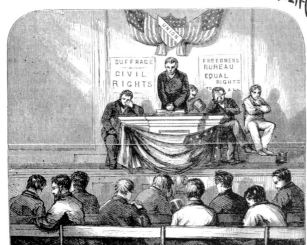

CONVENTION OR MASSACRE.

18 WHICH IS THE MORE ILLEGAL.

(?) "SLAVERY IS DEAD"? (?)
CIVIL RIGHTS BILL
AUCTION SALE
EMANCIPATION PROCLAMATION
JANUARY 1ST 1863.
ALL PERSONS HELD AS SLAVES WITHIN ANY STATES
UNITED STATES SHALL BE THEN THENCE FORWARD AND FOREVER FREE
A LINCOLN
H SEWARD
SLAVERY IS ABOLISHED BY THE STATES AND U. S. CONGRESS
"PUBLIC SALE"
JUSTICE
STATE RIGHTS.
THE LAND OF THE FREE.
Negroes Sold as a Punishment for Crime.
"PUBLIC SALE.—The undersigned will offer for sale, at the Court-house door in the City of Annapolis, at 11 o'clock A.M., on Saturday, the 22d of December, a negro man named Jno. Johnson, aged about 40 years. The said negro was convicted at the October term, 1866, of the Circuit Court of Ann Arundel County, of larceny, and sentenced to be sold. WM. BRYAN, Sheriff."
"BALTIMORE, DEC. 24.—Four negroes convicted of larceny, and ordered to be sold by Judge Magruder, at Annapolis, were sold on Saturday last."
1866
Negroes Whipped as a Punishment for Crime.
"On Monday last an order issued by Gen. Sickles, commanding this Department, was handed to Judge Fowle, by order of the Military Commander here, prohibiting infliction of corporal punishment. On Thursday a telegram from Gov. Worth, at Washington, was received by the same Judge, saying 'that the order was rescinded—you may proceed with the punishment.' Sheriff Ray then proceeded to inflict the punishment." —Raleigh (North Carolina) Standard of December 22, 1866.
Th. Nast.
THE HOME OF THE BRAVE.

19

BANCROFT THE ORATOR THAT HURT THE ENGLISHMEN'S FEELINGS.

MISS BATEMAN.

MARS AS STANTON. U.S

NORTH MISS KE

THE VETO. FREEDMEN

N.Y. TRIBUNE

MISS WENDELL PHILIPS AND HER ADOPTED CHILD.

OUR MARE. CITY HALL STABLE

MAX MARETZEK

GRAND MASQUERADE BALL GIVEN BY MR. MARETZEK

GNOR BELLINI.

PHOENIX.

BARNUMS AMERICAN MUSEUM.

WHO'S THIS? BOOTH THE PRINCE OF DENMARK

ALL ABOARD FOR IRELAND

LOOK OUT FOR THE TRAIN.

20

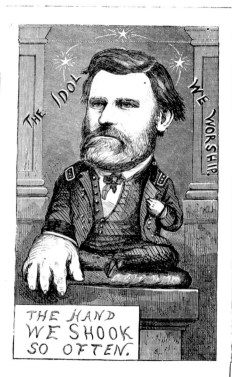

THE IDOL WE WORSHIP.

THE HAND WE SHOOK SO OFTEN.

Th. Nast.

R ARTIST Th. Nast

BEECHER THE C.S.A. RATTLESNAKE CHARMER.

C.S.A

DEAD DUCK.

A STUDY FROM NATURE BY ANDY JOHNSON.

THE POST

21

STRANGER THINGS HAVE HAPPENED.
HOLD ON, AND YOU MAY WALK OVER THE SLUGGISH ANIMAL UP THERE YET.

THE THIRD-TERM PANIC.

"An Ass, having put on the Lion's skin, roamed about in the Forest, and amused himself by frightening all the foolish Animals he met with in his wanderings."—SHAKSPEARE or BACON.

22

THE HAUNTED HOUSE; OR, THE "MURDERED" RAG BABY WILL NOT BE STILL.
SHAKE ITS GORY LOCKS AT THEM UNTIL THEY MAKE IT VANISH.

23

NEXT!

CIVILIZED BY THE BALLOT BOX.

MISUSE IT AND YOU WILL SUFFER.

THE BALLOT THE GREAT PROTECTOR OF THE AGE.

GIVE THE NATIVES A CHANCE, MR. CARL.
THE CHEAPEST AND QUICKEST WAY OF CIVILIZING THEM.

24

SLIPPERY SAM.

A ONE MAN POWER—PULLING THE STRINGS.

A Plaything in Governor Tilden's Hands.

POCKETING THE MISSING PLANK.

BUT THEY ARE SURE TO PUT THEIR FOOT IN IT SOME DAY.

26

THE CRADLE OF LIBERTY IN DANGER.

"Fee-Fi-Fo-Fum!" The Genie of Massachusetts smells Blue Blood.

A HARD FISH TO CATCH.

JOHN BULL TO SPAIN. "It's difficult Fishing here!"

27

HARPER'S WEEKLY.

A JOURNAL OF CIVILIZATION.

Vol. XXIII.—No. 1199.]   NEW YORK, SATURDAY, DECEMBER 20, 1879.   [SINGLE COPIES TEN CENTS.
$4.00 PER YEAR IN ADVANCE.

Entered according to Act of Congress, in the Year 1879, by Harper & Brothers, in the Office of the Librarian of Congress, at Washington.

BORROWED PLUMES—MR. JACKDAW CONKLING.

EAGLE. "Perhaps you would like to pluck me."

29

CAN THE LAW REACH HIM?—THE DWARF AND THE GIANT THIEF.

n. To enhance motivation, education

important. But motivation is mainly

most significant way to enhance

n Japan, many people are doing over

g that? For earning more money, for

ANDREW JOHNSON'S

RECONSTRUCTION,

AND

HOW IT WORKS.

OTHELLO. DOST THOU MOCK ME?
IAGO.   I MOCK YOU! NO, BY HEAVEN:
WOULD YOU WOULD BEAR YOUR FORTUNES LIKE A MAN.
—SHAKSPEARE.

AMPHITHEATRUM JOHNSONIANUM—MASSACRE OF THE INNOCENTS AT NEW ORLEANS, JULY 30, 1866   *32*

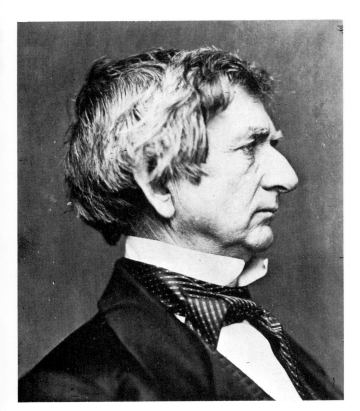

WILLIAM H. SEWARD

ANDREW JOHNSON

"We regard the Reconstruction Acts (so called) of Congress as usurpations, and unconstitutional, revolutionary, and void."—*Democratic Platform.*

WILKES BOOTH THE SECOND.

"If he is elected by unfair means, or use of illegal power—if he does not receive a majority of the three hundred and seventeen votes of the Electoral College, fairly cast—if he seeks to override a majority in America, *he dies before his term of office shall one-fourth expire,* and the party that would thus unjustly elevate him to power shall be strangled in the blood it cries for."—*The Democrat, Oct. 13, 1868.*

"THE TYRANNICAL MILITARY DESPOTISM OF OUR REPUBLIC"

"FATAL TO THE UNION AND THE CONSTITUTION," "THE NATIONAL STANDARD MUST BE BORNE IN FRONT OF THE COLUMN."
"O MY CONSTITUTION!" "IT MAKES ONES BLOOD BOIL IN EVERY ARTERY."
"DOES THE CONSTITUTION SAY THAT WE MUST CARRY A UNION FLAG?" "WHAT COULD BE MORE DEGRADING THAN TO CARRY THE AMERICAN FLAG!"

D. E. SICKLES MAJOR-GENERAL COMMANDING

"Charleston, S. C., April 20, 1869.—.... By some the order was therefore looked upon as an intrusion unjustifiable, if not tyrannical. These were in favor of an abandonment of the parade. Some of the most violent left the ranks and went home..... No objection, they thought, ought to be made, particularly as the Stonewall Fire Engine Company appeared on the ground in Confederate gray, and with a full-sized portrait of Stonewall Jackson carpeted over their engine."—Special Correspondent of the New York Herald.

35

"WHO GOES THERE?"—"A FRIEND."

"THAT'S WHAT'S THE MATTER."

Boss Tweed. "As long as I count the Votes, what are you going to do about it? say?"

37

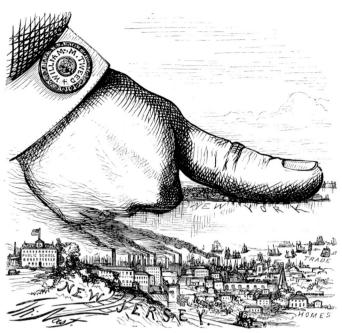

UNDER THE THUMB.

The Boss. "Well, what are you going to do about it?"

38

THE "BRAINS"

That achieved the Tammany Victory at the Rochester Democratic Convention.

39

"GROSS IRREGULARITY NOT 'FRAUDULENT.'"

Boss Sweed. "To make this *look straight* is the hardest job I ever had. What made Watson go sleigh-riding?"

40

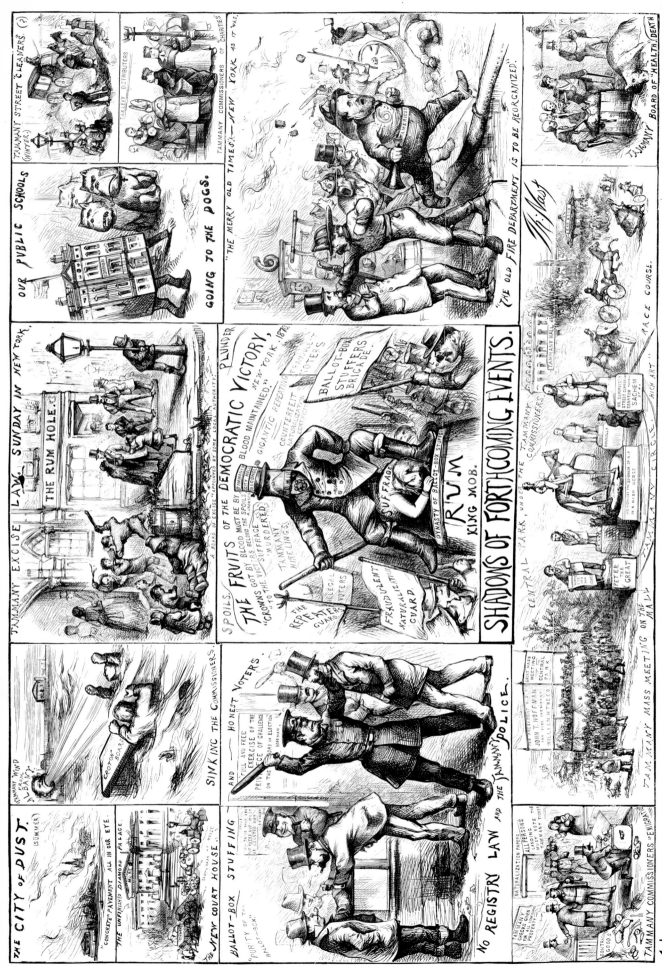

SHADOWS OF FORTHCOMING EVENTS.

N.Y. STATE LEGISLATURE

DEMOCRATIC FIGHT OVER THE SACKING, N.Y.

NEW YORK CITY TREASURY AND OFFICES

PUSH PUSH

THE NEW CHARTER FOR THE CITY OF NEW YORK

42

HAMLET. Whiles rank corruption, mining all within,
Infects unseen. Confess yourself to heaven;
Repent what's past; avoid what is to come.
QUEEN (TWEED). Oh, Hamlet! thou hast cleft my heart in twain.
HAMLET. Oh! throw away the worser part of it,
And live the purer with the other half.
ASSUME A VIRTUE, IF YOU HAVE IT NOT.—*Shakspeare.*

SENATOR TWEED IN A NEW RÔLE.

THREE BLIND MICE! SEE HOW THEY RUN!
THE *Times* CUT OFF THEIR TAILS WITH A CARVING-KNIFE.

43

TWEEDLEDEE AND SWEEDLEDUM.

(*A New Christmas Pantomime at the Tammany Hall.*)

CLOWN (*to* PANTALOON). "Let's Blind them with *this*, and then take *some more*."

44

THE NEW BOARD OF EDUCATION.

SOWING THE SEED, WITH AN EYE TO THE HARVEST.

45

NOT A BAILABLE CASE.

THE GREAT AMERICAN FARMER TROUBLED WITH THE MILK OF HUMAN KINDNESS AGAIN.

"*We have scrupulously refrained from the intemperate and indiscriminate style of attack in which the* TIMES *has of late profusely indulged, because words thus used lose their force, and because we did not have proofs to warrant charges which, nevertheless, we have often believed to be true.*"
—N. Y. Tribune, July 21.

46

"WHO STOLE THE PEOPLE'S MONEY?"—DO TELL. N.Y.TIMES.

'TWAS HIM.

THE AMERICAN RIVER GANGES.

THE PRIESTS AND THE CHILDREN.—[See Page 915.]

48

A GROUP OF VULTURES WAITING FOR THE STORM TO "BLOW OVER."—"LET US *PREY.*"

49

50

NEXT!

51

GOING THROUGH THE FORM OF UNIVERSAL SUFFRAGE.

Boss. "You have the *Liberty* of *Voting* for any one you please; but we have the *Liberty* of *Counting* in any one we please."

"Do your Duty as Citizens, and leave the rest to take its course."—*New York Times.*

THE TAMMANY TIGER LOOSE.—"What are you going to do about it?"

52

"WHAT ARE YOU LAUGHING AT? TO THE VICTOR BELONG THE SPOILS."

SOMETHING THAT DID BLOW OVER—NOVEMBER 7, 1871.

54

THE ARREST OF "BOSS" TWEED—ANOTHER GOOD JOKE.

THE SHADOW OF JUSTICE. "I'LL MAKE SOME OF YOU CRY YET."

"Sheriff BRENNAN merely nodded to Mr. TWEED, bade him 'Good-day,' and laying his hand tenderly on his shoulder, said, laughingly, 'You're my man!' It seemed like a deliciously cool joke, and, judging from the faces, it was."—*New York Tribune*.

55

"STONE WALLS DO NOT A PRISON MAKE."—*Old Song.*

A Prophecy from HARPER'S WEEKLY of January 6, 1872.

"OUR MARE STILL LIVES."

58

"ET TU, BRUTE?—THEN FALL, CÆSAR."

59

THE FINGER OF SCORN

SHALL FOLLOW THEM, IF LAW (SOMETIMES CALLED JUSTICE) CAN NOT.

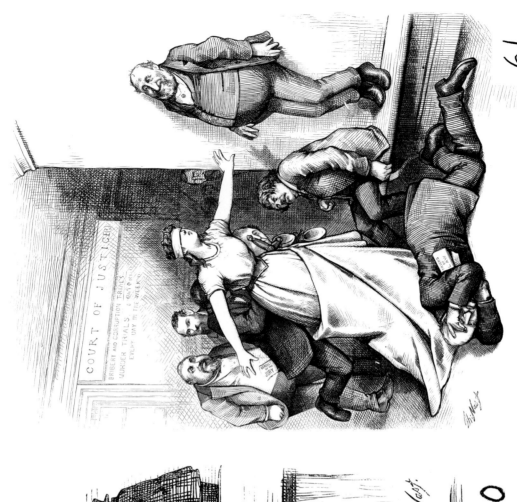

BLINDMAN'S-BUFF.

How long will this Game last?

61

JANUARY 1, 1873.

The last of the Mare Disease with which this City has been so much afflicted

60

THE CAT'S-PAW.—ANY THING TO GET CHESTNUTS.

62

"SAVE ME FROM MY TOBACCO PARTNER!"

"OLD HONESTY." "Do, Somebody, arrest him, or I shall never get to the White House!"

64

"IN MY MIND'S EYE."

GHOST OF —— "I could a tale unfold, whose lightest word   Thy knotted and combined locks to part,
        Would harrow up thy soul; freeze thy young blood;   And each particular hair to stand on end,
        Make thy two eyes, like stars, start from their spheres;   Like quills upon the fretful porcupine."—SHAKSPEARE.

GRANT'S STRATEGY.

U. S. G.—"*Confound those bubbles!—they all burst. I really thought that last one would knock him over: but that's gone, too.*"

"*Transportation to this Convention was obtained and paid for by the Grant people. My own, and those of five others, each representing a district in Pennsylvania, I procured in the office of the Grant State Central Committee of Pennsylvania, at Philadelphia. The band of music that accompanied us was furnished and paid for by the same Grant people, and our little banner is the same that designated the seats in the Radical Convention of the 5th of June, of the Pennsylvania delegation, that nominated U. S. Grant.*"—W. FISK CONRAD, Delegate to the Louisville Convention from the 17th Pennsylvania District.

65

66

"SATAN, DON'T GET THEE BEHIND ME!"—ANY THING TO GET POSSESSION.

THE LAST SHOT OF THE HONORABLE SENATOR FROM MASSACHUSETTS.—HE PULLED THE LONG-BOW ONCE TOO OFTEN.

WHAT H— G— KNOWS ABOUT BAILING.

68

WHAT H. G. KNOWS ABOUT THRASHING.

And now "He comes among us to ask that we adopt *Him* as our Party Chief."—*New York World,* June 6, 1872.

DIOGENES HAS FOUND THE *HONEST MAN.*—(WHICH IS *DIOGENES,* AND WHICH IS THE *HONEST MAN?*)

"As soon as the news that GREELEY and BROWN had been nominated was received, bunting was unfurled from every flag-staff on the *City Hall.* In the *City Hall Park* was displayed a large banner, bearing the inscription: 'TAMMANY RESPONDS TO THE NOMINATIONS OF THE NATIONAL CONVENTION AT BALTIMORE.'"—*New York Tribune,* July 11, 1872.

71

BRINGING THE THING HOME.—(Dedicated to the Baltimore Convention.)

"When the Rebellious Traitors are overwhelmed in the Field, and scattered like Leaves before an angry Wind, it must not be to return to *Peaceful and Contented Homes. They must find Poverty at their Fire-sides, and see Privation in the Anxious Eyes of Mothers and the Rags of Children.*"—*New York Tribune*, November 26, 1860.

BALTIMORE 1861—1872.
"Let us Clasp Hands over the Bloody Chasm."

72

"OLD HONESTY" AMONG THE RUINS OF TAMMANY.

73

THE NEW ORGAN- (we beg the "Tribune's" pardon) -IZATION ON ITS "NEW DEPARTURE."—ANY THING TO GET VOTES.

75

"SHYLOCK, WE WOULD HAVE MONEYS AND VOTES."

This is a white man's
government.

Auction block.

Hunting down with
blood-hounds.

A negro has no rights
which a white man is
bound to respect.

Slavery.

Whipping-post.

New York riots.

Negroes hung at lamp-
posts.

Attempt to introduce
pestilence in the North.

Attempt to burn Northern
cities.

Burning of colored orphan
asylum.

New Orleans and Memphis
massacres.

Belle Isle and Andersonville
atrocities.

Assassination of Lincoln.

Ku-klux outrages to Unionists,
white and black.

Burning of Freedmen's schools.

Whipping and shooting of teach-
ers.

Repudiation.

Fort Pillow massacre, approved
by Congress of Confederate States
of America.

KU-KLUX.

THE RULE OF TAMMANY RING.
WHOLESALE FRAUD.
CORRUPTION.
NO CITIZEN HAD ANY RIGHTS THAT A TAMMANY ROUGH
WAS BOUND TO RESPECT.
CORRUPT JUDICIARY—CARDOZO, BARNARD, AND M'CUNN.
FRAUDULENT AND ILLEGAL VOTING.
BRIBERY.
COUNTING OUT THE VOTES OF CITIZENS.
RIOT AND BLOODSHED.

NAMES NOT TO BE FORGOTTEN:
TWEED, SWEENY, CONNOLLY, and HALL.

SLAVERY

76

THE WHITED SEPULCHRE.
COVERING THE MONUMENT OF INFAMY WITH HIS WHITE HAT AND COAT.

77

"LET US CLASP HANDS OVER THE BLOODY CHASM."—HORACE GREELEY.

New-York Tribune

NEW SERIES.   NEW-YORK, WEDNESDAY, NOVEMBER 6, 1872.   DEAR AT ANY PRICE

78

"WE ARE ON THE HOME STRETCH."—*New York Tribune*, October 9, 1872.

THE MEETING OF NAST AND WATTERSON IN CENTRAL JERSEY.—[Drawn on the Spot.]

"Mr. Watterson was so much overcome with joy at the sight of Nast that he felt strongly impelled to rush forward and throw his arms about the neck of the man whom he had traveled so far to find. 'The effort of restraint,' says Mr. Watterson, 'at that supreme moment of my journey, was positively painful; but in presence of those who certainly would have been unsympathetic, and possibly might have been hostile, the restraint was essential.' Then the Kentuckian advanced and saluted the adventurous Jerseyman. 'Nast, I presume?' The artistic stranger replied, simply, 'Yes;' but the more effusive Kentuckian exclaimed, 'Thank goodness that I have been permitted to see you!' The long-lost artist calmly rejoined, 'It is quite a wonderful event."—Copyright, 1881, Louisville Courier-Journal.

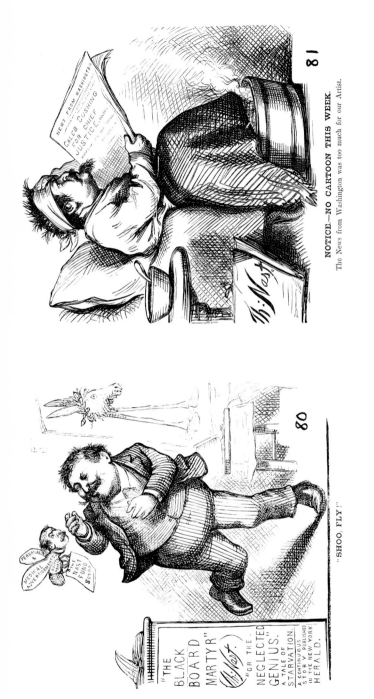

"THE BLACK BOARD MARTYR"
"OR THE NEGLECTED GENIUS."
A TALE OF STARVATION.
A CONTINUOUS STORY PUBLISHED IN THE NEW YORK HERALD.

80

"SHOO, FLY!"

NEWS FROM WASHINGTON
CALEB CUSHING FOR CHIEF JUSTICE

81

NOTICE.—NO CARTOON THIS WEEK.

The News from Washington was too much for our Artist.

THE SENATORIAL CABAL DESTROYED.
SHAM REFORM EXPOSED.
THE GREELEY TRIUMPH POSTPONED.
FOR THE PRESENT THE BLACK MOVEMENT SEEMS CRUSHED.

NEW YORK TIMES

TRIBUNE

GRANT'S VICTORY

TAMMANY RING FORCED.
REFORM TAMMANY DEAD.
K.K.K. DEAD.
THE GREELEY PILL NO GO.

HARPERS WEEKLY SKETCHES

82

OUR ARTIST'S OCCUPATION GONE.

Th. Nast. "It's all very funny to you; but what am I to do now?"

U.S. SENATE

SPEECHES

83

THE WHIRLIGIG OF TIME.

THE BACK-PAY I OBJECT TO.
THE INCREASED SALARY IS JUST AND OUGHT NOT TO BE REDUCED BACK TO THE ORIGINAL PITIFUL FIGURE, HAND OVER THE BACK PAY.
U. SAM.

TO BACK PAY

84

Peculiar position of some Members when asked to refund the Back-Pay Grab.

85

IT STRUCK (IN BLOWING OVER).—PICKING EVEN THE POOR SOLDIERS' BONES TO FEATHER THEIR NEST.

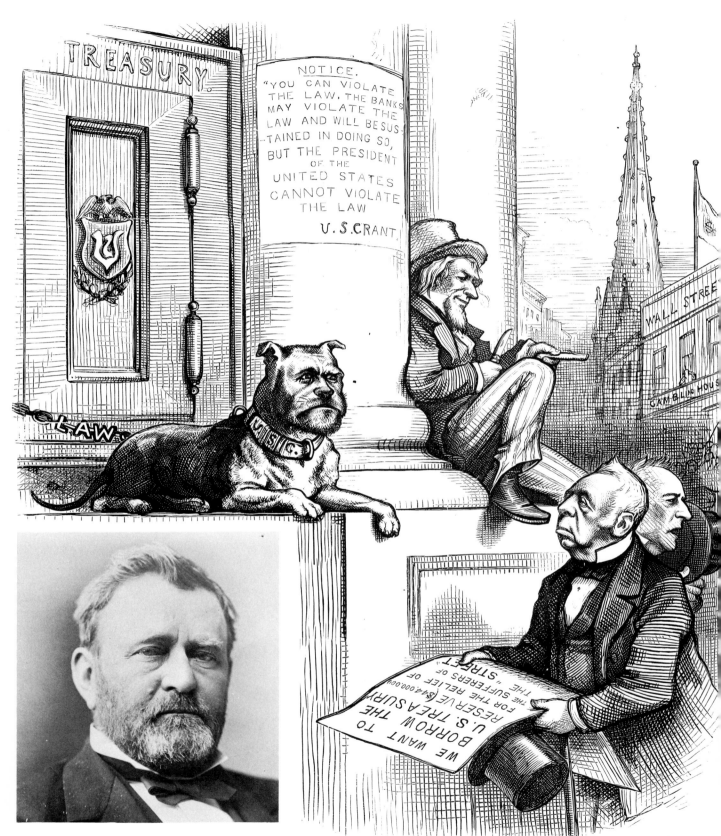

KEEPING THE MONEY WHERE IT WILL DO MOST GOOD.

UNCLE SAM. "Look out, boys, they say he's a Cæsar (seiz-er)."

86

87

EVERY PUBLIC QUESTION WITH AN EYE ONLY TO THE PUBLIC GOOD.

"Well, the wickedness of all of it is, not that these men were bribed or corruptly influenced, but that they betrayed the trust of the people, deceived their constituents, and by their evasions and falsehoods confessed the transaction to be disgraceful."—*New York Tribune*, February 14, 1873.

Justice (to the Saints of the Press). "Let him that has not betrayed the trust of the People, and is without stain, cast the first stone."

THE NATION IS SICK OF DIRTY "GREAT MEN—PUBLIC MEN AND FAMOUS MEN."

MEMBERS OF THE PRESS KEEP CLEAN (IF YOU CAN) FOR THE SAKE OF THE EXAMPLE

FOR THE SAKE OF CHRISTIANITY. KEEP THE PUBLIC PURE.

DEAD HEAD FRAUDS OUGHT TO BE WASHED OUT.

REFORMERS WASH OUT YOUR OLD STAINS

NOTICE. LET EVERY TUB STAND ON ITS OWN BOTTOM.

KEEP CLEAN AND PURE.

MAKE A CLEAN BREAST OF IT.

CLEANLINESS IS NEXT TO GODLINESS.

"OUT DAMNED (CORRUPTION) SPOT." "THERE'S THE RUB."

CLEAN LINEN

HONESTY.—DUTY.

CAPACITY.—INTELLIGENCE.

EDUCATION.

KEEP THE BENCH PURE.

CIVIL SERVICE SOAP. THE BOARD OF HEALTH.

PUBLIC CORRUPTION
THE PRESS RING
CANAL RING
WHISKEY RING
INDIAN RING

INTERNAL REVENUE FRAUDS
BRIBERY
PACIFIC MAIL SUBSIDY
TREASURY FRAUDS
CREDIT MOBILIER FRAUDS
EMBEZZLEMENT
CUSTOM HOUSE FRAUDS
POST OFFICE FRAUDS
BACK PAY
SAVINGS BANKS FRAUDS

TAMMANY HALL 1872.

TAMMANY

RING

88

THIS TUB HAS NO BOTTOM TO STAND ON.

JUSTICE (*chief washer-woman*). "The bottom fell out, and the rest came tumbling after."

89

THE CROWNING INSULT TO HIM WHO OCCUPIES THE PRESIDENTIAL CHAIR.

REPUBLICAN "SIMPLICITY."

THE GOOD AND BAD SPIRITS AT WAR.

"Woman [Joan of Arc], do what thou canst to save our honors. Drive them from the country, and be immortalized."—*Shakspeare.*

90

"HALT!"

"This is not the way 'to repress corruption and to initiate the Negroes into the ways of honest and orderly government.'"

93

THE SAME OLD PIRATE AFLOAT AGAIN.—[See Page 778.]

A GENERAL BLOW UP—DEAD ASSES KICKING A LIVE LION.

A LEGITIMATE QUESTION ABOUT HOME RULE.—[See Article, "A Divided Allegiance," Page 218.]

U. S. Republic. "To whom do you owe your first allegiance?"
Hon. F. Kernan (*From New York* [?]). "This is a very embarrassing position to be placed in."

96

HARPERS WEEKLY

A JOURNAL OF CIVILIZATION

NEW YORK, SATURDAY, OCTOBER 9, 1875.

VOL. XIX.—No. 980.

WITH A SUPPLEMENT.
PRICE TEN CENTS.

Entered according to Act of Congress, in the Year 1875, by Harper & Brothers, in the Office of the Librarian of Congress, at Washington.

"HOLY MURDER!!!"
GOVERNOR TILDEN AND THE OHIO RAG BABY.

95

OUR MODERN CANUTE AT LONG BRANCH.

U. S. G. "I can no more proclaim myself Cæsar than I can compel the Atlantic Ocean to recede, and you know it."

97

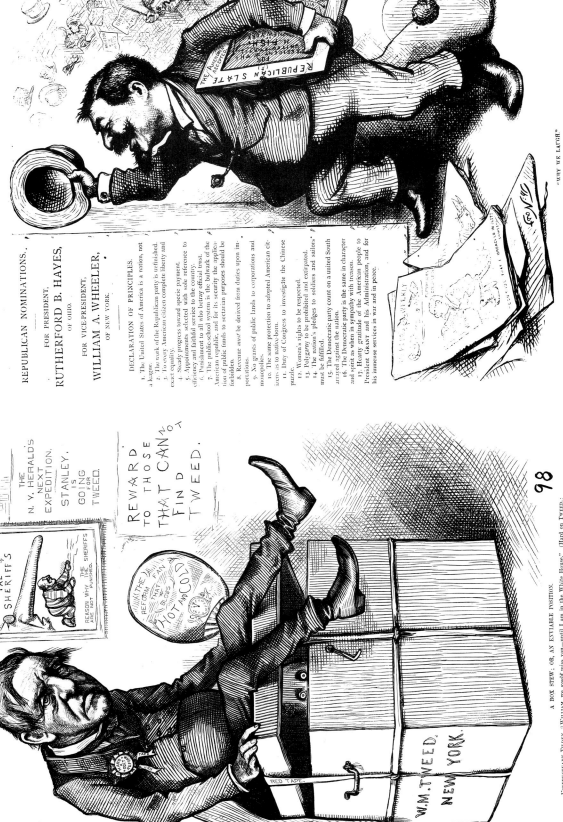

REPUBLICAN NOMINATIONS.

FOR PRESIDENT,
RUTHERFORD B. HAYES,
OF OHIO.

FOR VICE-PRESIDENT,
WILLIAM A. WHEELER,
OF NEW YORK.

DECLARATION OF PRINCIPLES.

1. The United States of America is a nation, not a league.

2. The work of the Republican party is unfinished.

3. To every American citizen complete liberty and exact equality.

4. Steady progress toward specie payment.

5. Appointments selected with sole reference to efficiency and faithful service to the country.

6. Punishment to all who betray official trust.

7. The public-school system is the bulwark of the American republic, and for its security the application of public funds to sectarian purposes should be forbidden.

8. Revenue *must* be derived from duties upon importations.

9. No grants of public lands to corporations and monopolies.

10. The same protection to adopted American citizens as to native-born.

11. Duty of Congress to investigate the Chinese puzzle.

12. Women's rights to be respected.

13. Polygamy to be prohibited and extirpated.

14. The nation's pledges to soldiers and sailors' must be fulfilled.

15. The Democratic party count on a united South arrayed against the nation.

16. The Democratic party is the same in character and spirit as when in sympathy with treason.

17. Hearty gratitude of the American people to President GRANT and his Administration, and for his immense services in war and in peace.

"WHY WE LAUGH."

99

THE N. Y. HERALD'S
NEXT EXPEDITION.
STANLEY
IS
GOING
FOR TWEED.

THE SHERIFF'S
REASON WHY THE SHERIFFS ARE NOT PUNISHED.

REFORM THAT FAN THAT BLOWS HOT AND COLD

REWARD
TO THOSE
THAT CANNOT
FIND TWEED.

W.M. TWEED.
NEW YORK.

RED TAPE.

98

A BOX STEW; OR, AN ENVIABLE POSITION.

USUFRUCTUARY TILDEN. "WILLIAM, we *would* miss you—until I am in the White House." (Hard on TWEED.)

100

STRUCK—AT SEA.

IF IT HAD NOT BEEN FOR THAT HAZE (HAYES), THEY COULD HAVE STEERED CLEAR OF THE ICEBERG.

101

TILDEN'S "WOLF AT THE DOOR, GAUNT AND HUNGRY."—DON'T LET HIM IN.

102

"THE REPUBLIC IN DANGER."

SPRING CHICKEN (*cackling to Centennial Eagle*). "Dear Mr. Eagle, I am seriously alarmed for your safety. Your *Constitution* is in danger of breaking down; and even if that Blackbird does not destroy you, I am afraid that my Father on the opposite Cliff will peck you to pieces. You had better take refuge under the Shelter of My Wing."

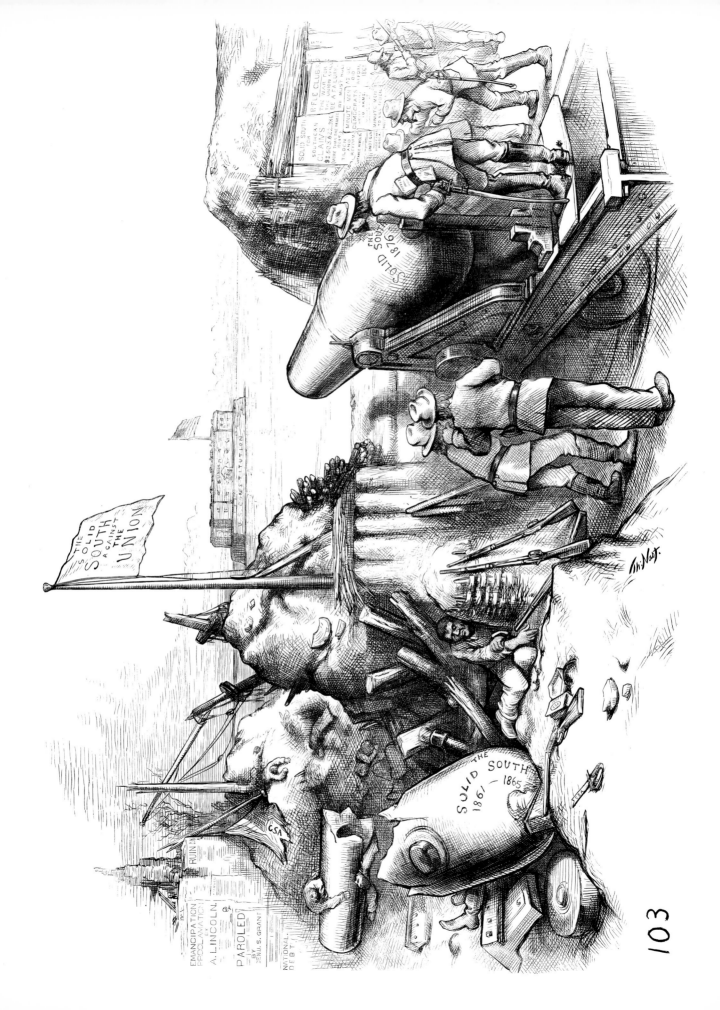

103

WAITING.

105

"AMNESTY", OR THE END OF THE PEACEFUL (DEMOCRATIC) TIGER.

104

THEY BOTH LIE TOGETHER IN THE WASHINGTON ARENA.

DEMOCRATIC TIGER. " I have reformed, and am tame now."

REPUBLICAN LAMB. " I—I believe it !"

106

BY REPEALING THEY RESUME—BY RESUMING THEY REPEAL.

Extremes have met, and now you can't tell which is which.

THE ELASTIC DEMOCRATIC (DEFORMED) TIGER.

They pull together so very nicely.

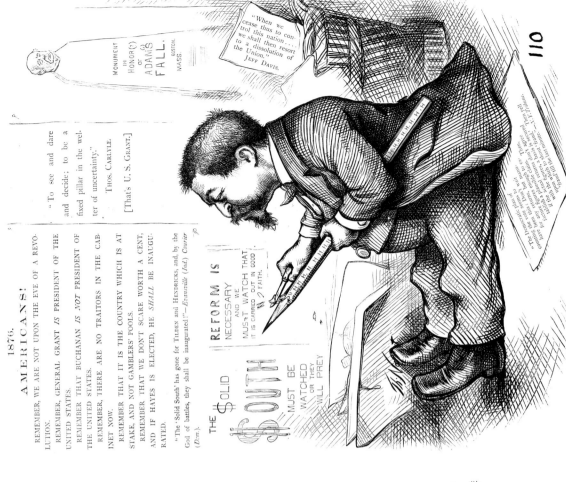

1876.

AMERICANS!

REMEMBER, WE ARE NOT UPON THE EVE OF A REVOLUTION.

REMEMBER, GENERAL GRANT *IS* PRESIDENT OF THE UNITED STATES.

REMEMBER THAT BUCHANAN *IS NOT* PRESIDENT OF THE UNITED STATES.

REMEMBER, THERE ARE NO TRAITORS IN THE CABINET NOW.

REMEMBER THAT IT IS THE COUNTRY WHICH IS AT STAKE, AND NOT GAMBLERS' POOLS.

REMEMBER THAT WE DON'T SCARE WORTH A CENT, AND IF HAYES IS ELECTED, HE *SHALL* BE INAUGURATED.

"The 'Solid South' has gone for TILDEN and HENDRICKS, and, by the God of battles, they shall be inaugurated!"—*Evansville (Ind.) Courier (Dem.).*

"To see and dare and decide; to be a fixed pillar in the welter of uncertainty."
THOS. CARLYLE.

[That's U. S. GRANT.]

MONUMENT IN HONOR OF ADAMS FALL. BOSTON. MASS.

"When we cease thus to control this nation . . . . we shall then resort to a dissolution of the Union."
JEFF DAVIS.

THE $OLID $OUTH

MUST BE WATCHED OR THEY WILL PREY

REFORM IS NECESSARY AND WE MUST WATCH THAT IT IS CARRIED OUT IN GOOD FAITH.

NO REST FOR THE WICKED—SENTENCED TO MORE HARD LABOR.

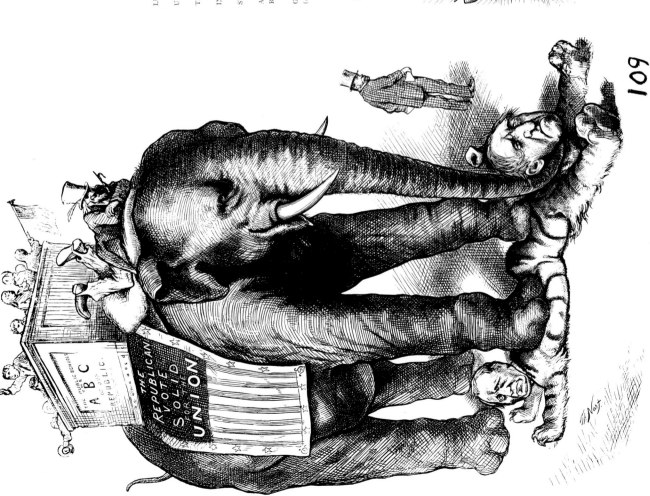

THE REPUBLICAN VOTE SOLID FOR THE UNION

PUBLIC SCHOOLS A B C REPUBLIC

THE ELEPHANT WALKS AROUND—AND THE "STILL HUNT" IS NEARLY OVER

IN MEMORIAM—OUR CIVIL SERVICE AS IT WAS.

"THE BEST OF FRIENDS MUST PART."

BUT THEIR DESTINATION IS NOT DECIDED YET, BY D. D. FIELD, COUNSEL OF FISK, GOULD, TWEED, TILDEN, & CO.

HARPER'S WEEKLY.

JOURNAL OF CIVILIZATION.

Vol. XXI.—No. 1062.]   NEW YORK, SATURDAY, MAY 5, 1877.   [WITH A SUPPLEMENT.
PRICE TEN CENTS.

Entered according to Act of Congress, in the Year 1877, by Harper & Brothers, in the Office of the Librarian of Congress, at Washington.

PUBLIC NOTICE.
"WATCH AND PRAY."
STAND BACK AND
GIVE THE PRESIDENT'S
POLICY A CHANCE.

GEN. DISPOSITION.

BLUE ROOM
IN THE
WHITE HOUSE.

113

"NAY, PATIENCE, OR WE BREAK THE SINEWS."—Shakspeare.
U. S. "Our Artist must keep cool, and sit down, and see how it works."

THE FIRST STEP TOWARD NATIONAL BANKRUPTCY.

THE TWO GEORGES.

GEORGE III. TO GEORGE WASHINGTON. "I say, George—Daddy—is that the free and enlightened Cherub for whom you fought? Don't you think you had better write another Farewell Address to him?"

116

TAKING A REST (?)—DIE WACHT AM—BISMARCK.

SOCIAL SCIENCE SOLVED.

THE MODERN ARCHIMEDES. *"Eureka! Eureka!"*

"Constant Vigilance" (committee) "is the price of Liberty" in San Francisco.

118

A MATTER OF TASTE.

CONFUCIUS. "How can Christians stomach such dirt?"

CIPHER MUMM(ER)Y.

EXHUMED BY THE NEW YORK TRIBUNE.—[SEE PAGE 875.]

119

THE MILLENNIUM.
THE TIGER AND THE LAMB LIE TOGETHER.

OUR PATIENT ARTIST.

THE LIGHTNING SPEED OF HONESTY.

122

THE WHOLE COUNTRY IS GOING TO THE DOGS

OUT OF OFFICE

SENATOR THURMAN'S SPEECH AT COLUMBUS, OHIO, APRIL 24.

"It has been said that every Presidential election is a crisis in this Republic, and though it might be doubted whether in the past that remark is so absolutely true that there was no exception to it, yet it must be admitted that in later years every Presidential election in fact has been a crisis in our affairs, and no one can tell how long it may thus continue to be. But of one thing I think we may be absolutely certain, and that is, that the Presidental election of 1880 will be regarded, as long as the history of this country shall be read and studied, as a crisis in the Republic. And why do I say this? I am not accustomed, it is not my wont, to magnify things. Why, then, do I say that this is a crisis in public affairs? Because, my friends, in my serious judgment, the election this year will go far to determine whether substantial liberty and substantial free institutions shall longer continue in America ... We need a stronger Government.... In my judgment the great question which is to be solved is whether or no the strength of our Government in the future shall come from the affections of the people, or whether it shall be that strength that despots and despots alone employ."

123

OUR REPUBLIC IS ALWAYS "GOING TO THE DOGS"—ACCORDING TO THOSE WHO CAN NOT RUN IT.

GENERAL HANCOCK GULLIVER, HOW DO YOU LIKE IT AS FAR AS YOU'VE GOT?

"I confess I was often tempted, while they were passing backward and forward on my body, to seize forty or fifty of the first that came in my reach, and dash them against the ground. But the remembrance of what I had felt, which probably might not be the worst they could do, and the promise of honor I made them, for so I interpreted my submissive behavior, soon drove out these imaginations. . . . However, in my thoughts I could not sufficiently wonder at the intrepidity of these diminutive mortals, who durst venture to mount and walk upon my body, while one of my hands was at liberty, without trembling at the very sight of so prodigious a creature as I must appear to them."

124

125

AS SOLID AND DEFIANT AS EVER.

"THE LAST VESTIGE OF THE WAR LEGISLATION SHALL BE SWEPT FROM THE STATUTE BOOK."
SOLID SOUTH.

"THE NATIONAL DEBT SHALL BE WIPED OUT."
SOLID SOUTH.

"THE SOUTHERN DEBT MUST BE PAID SOMEHOW."
SOLID SOUTH.

"ALL UNION SOLDIERS MUST GO."
SOLID SOUTH.

SOLID (SOUTHERN) SENTIMENT.

ROBERT TOOMBS TO A FRIEND IN WASHINGTON.

" I AM as positive that HANCOCK will be elected as I am that there is a God in the heavens. You say that he is a Yankee. Well, I know that; and I know, too, that his sword has pierced the breast of many a gallant man in gray. But what are we to do? We can not put in one of our own men this time, and have to take a 'Yank.' That being the case, let us take one who is less 'blue-bellied' than the most of them. You may depend upon it, sir, that, 'Yank' or no 'Yank,' if elected, the old boys of the South will see that HANCOCK does the fair thing by them. In other words, he will run the machine to suit them, or they will run the thing themselves. They are not going to be played with any longer. If you hear any man say that HANCOCK can not carry all of the South, you may put him down as a d—— fool."

126

HE WILL BE GULLIVER IN THE HANDS OF THE BROBDINGNAGIANS.

BROBDINGNAG TOOMBS. "You may depend upon it, sir, that, 'Yank' or no 'Yank,' we will 'yank' you!"

127

HARD (*UP*) MONEY CAMPAIGN.

"Hang it, General, it's only Soft Soap!"

THE WIDOW'S WANTS.

"Well, what do you want, my sweet one? Don't be bashful."

A FINANCIAL MISTAKE.

GENERAL WEST-OFF HALFCOCK—KISSING "SOFT" BABIES IS SURE TO OFFEND "HARD" FATHERS.

HARPER'S WEEKLY.

A JOURNAL OF CIVILIZATION

Vol. XXV.—No. 1265.] NEW YORK, SATURDAY, MARCH 26, 1881. [SINGLE COPIES TEN CENTS. $4.00 PER YEAR IN ADVANCE.

Entered according to Act of Congress, in the Year 1881, by Harper & Brothers, in the Office of the Librarian of Congress, at Washington.

THE REAL CONNECTING LINK—THIS LOOKS LIKE BUSINESS.

131

WOMEN WILL NEVER BE STATESMEN.

PAT. "Where's the dinner?"
WIFE. "Ah! since ye've had stiddy wurrk, haven't ye had splindid dinners? and now yer always talking about change, change, change, and sure I thought I'd give ye wan."

132

NOW THEN, BUTT AWAY!

"A Bull, escaping from a Tiger, entered a cave which some shepherds had lately occupied. A he-Goat was left in it, who sharply attacked him with his horns. The Bull quietly addressed him: 'Butt away as much as you will. I have no fear of you, but of the Tiger. Let that monster go, and I will soon let you know what is the respective strength of a Goat and a Bull.'" A FABLE

HARPER'S WEEKLY.
JOURNAL OF CIVILIZATION.

VOL. XXV.—No. 1275.
Copyright, 1881, by HARPER & BROTHERS.

NEW YORK, SATURDAY, JUNE 4, 1881.

TEN CENTS A COPY.
$4.00 PER YEAR, IN ADVANCE.

133

135

THE CIVILIZATION OF BLAINE.

JOHN CONFUCIUS. "Am I not a Man and a Brother?"

134

THE SACRED ELEPHANT.

THIS ANIMAL IS SURE TO WIN, IF IT IS ONLY KEPT PURE AND CLEAN, AND HAS NOT TOO *HEAVY A LOAD TO CARRY.*

IS THIS "THE TRUE AMERICAN POLICY"?

SIR KNIGHT (*on his knees again*). "Yes, my letter of acceptance is as gentle as a sucking dove; but when I get in, I'll screech like an AMERICAN WAR-EAGLE, and I'll twist the British lion's tail for you; I'll protect you from British dungeons after you've killed innocent women and children with dynamite. Who could do more for you?"

GLORYING IN THEIR SHAME.
THE THICK-SKINNED ANIMAL GOING AROUND THE CIRCLE.

TRYING TO BULLY AND BROWBEAT EACH OTHER.
Mr. Blaine (*to* Mr. Badger Belmont). "I hope you will treat me as a gentleman. I am not in a police court to be BADGERED."

139

THE "GREAT AMERICAN" GAME OF PUBLIC OFFICE FOR PRIVATE GAIN.

This is not "*Protection*"; this is *very* "*Free Trade*" with the people's money.

140

THE SELF-CONVICTED KNIGHT.

YESTERDAY

He prayed on his knees for the return of his letters, for the sake of his wife and six children, and declared that if the committee should get hold of this communication it would sink him immediately and ruin him forever.

TO-DAY

He says there is not a word in those letters which is not entirely consistent with the most scrupulous integrity and honor, and hopes that every Republican paper in the United States will publish the letters in full.

141

"TAMMANY HALL IS GOING TO THE INAUGURATION."—*News.*
THEY CAN'T HELP THEMSELVES.

142

KEEP HER HEAD STRAIGHT FOR CIVIL-SERVICE REFORM.
NEW YORK. "Captain, Ohio tumbled overboard."
CAPTAIN CLEVELAND. "*I can't stop now.*"

ANARCHISTS' DRILL, NEW TACTICS.

GENERALISSIMO. "Double quick, under the bed, march!"

LIBERTY (to go if you do not like the institutions of our Republic) **OR** (commit murder and you will be punished with) **DEATH.**

THE PRESIDENT WAS ELECTED UPON THAT PLATFORM.

TAMMANY CHIEF. "I can not tell a lie; I want to cut it down with my little hatchet."

A POPULAR GAME: TWEED IN THE CORNER.

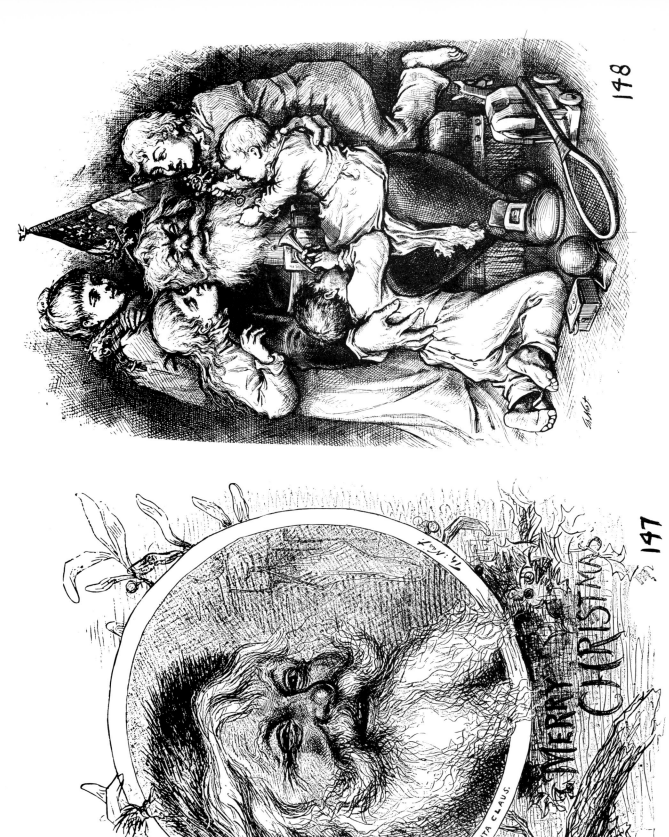

MERRY CHRISTMAS.

SANTA CLAUS.

MERRY CHRISTMAS

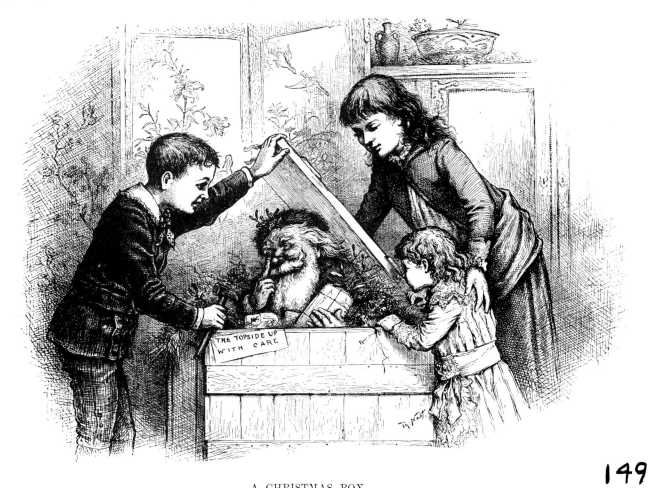

A CHRISTMAS BOX.

149

"ANOTHER STOCKING TO FILL."

150

MERRY OLD SANTA CLAUS.

CHRISTMAS IN CAMP.

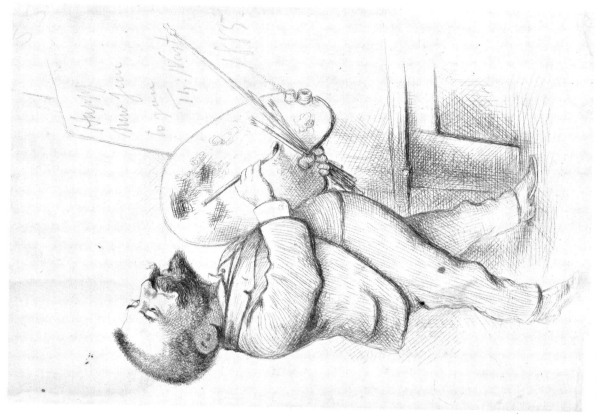

154

153

Last Christmas Wash Drawing

By Thomas Nast — 1900